The Wheel of Wealth
(An Entrepreneur's Action Guide)

Do These Things and You Will Make Big Money

Clay Clark

www.TotalPublishingAndMedia.com

ISBN: 978-1-937829-37-7

Testimonials:

"You certainly were the on-site leader that we needed for this calling campaign. By watching you work with these students and seeing the result, I became reassured that hiring you to do exactly what you did was the right thing to do. Your team brought in over $120K in gifts and pledges, which may be an all-time O.R.U. phonathon record! But I'll have more for you later. Again, thanks for everything...and don't drink too much Red Bull!"

Jesse D. Pisors, B.A. (1996) M.A. (2005)
Director of Alumni & Ministerial Relations and Annual Fund
Oral Roberts University

"Hi Clay. You have no idea how you blessed me with our conversation and the book recommendations. When I was in Tulsa, the Brazilian government made a sudden change in the regulations for the housing market that drove a lot of people out of business. We pretty much had to reinvent our business to survive. February through June were not fun.... However, God blessed us and we were able to survive and prosper. We have now about twenty employees working on three different construction sites. The principles in the books you recommended and the ones I 'caught' during our conversation have helped me a lot! I often tell my wife: 'If Clay Clark can run five businesses, then why can't I run a business and a ministry?" You have been an inspiration! Thanks my friend!"

In Him,
Rubens Cunha
Brazilian Missionary

"Hi Clay! Just had to start your Monday morning (oops, I forgot, your day is half over b.c I know you are up at 5:00am on Mondays preparing for your week!)....Anyway, with some GREAT NEWS!! Sweet Bottom, LLC entered a the 5th Annual Business Plan Competition at the Institute for Entrepreneurial Leadership in New Jersey. Guess what, we were a FINALIST! We were so excited for the exposure for our company. I had to fly up there this past Thursday and we had to deliver a 3 minute pitch to the judges, investors, entrepreneurs, community members, etc. We nailed it!

We WON the entire competition! A prize package valued at $30,000! Attached photo shows our enthusiasm! Just wanted to say thank you again, for your inspiration, and long distance support! You really impacted me that day at the Mount Pleasant Business Association on what one individual can accomplish in this world-gotta love capitalism! Thank you, Shawna, for arranging Clay to speak at our Expo! Have a great day!"

Michele L.
VP Business Development
Sweet Bottom Cookies

"(Within 2 months) my percentage of success on calls is drastically improving by using humor (4 new contracts with 5 calls). We've increased our profits by $2,800 per week (12K per month of gross income). We are above 1,100 staffing hours, we had been stuck at 700. The procedures make me feel better. We are not there yet, but we are getting close. We almost have all of our templates for client responses written. Are scripts are almost uniform. My way of thinking is changing and I am looking for ways to connect with people of influence. Our consistency is getting better. I am becoming a better manager and much more confident."

Cory M.
CEO of TES

"I attended the afternoon session of your Time Management session at the Permian Basin Regional Planning Commission and I was blown away! Thank you so much. I was truly inspired. I now know what I want to do and how I can find the time to do it! Thank you."

Thank you again,
Melissa Z.
Permian Basin Regional Planning Commission
Time Management and Stress Management Seminar Attendee

"Hey Clay. Thanks for all your help last year, we've done a lot of work, reading and investing and the results are truly amazing. Our best staff ever, continuous increases, and overall happiness like never before (and yes more profitable than in years and in a down economy)! I feel like we now have entirely new understanding on the importance of culture in the workplace. Do you have any more books you could recommend?!
Thanks again Clay!"

Thanks,
Dave B.
Maytag Store Owner

"I own Facchianos Bridal and Formal Attire and have had to pay thousands of dollars in the past to have websites that were subpar and not what I needed for my business until Clay taught me how to do it myself. Now my company website comes up on the search engines in the first three searches.

It has changed my business overnight on how many times our phone rings. It can change the life of your business to be in control of your website."

Jennifer Thompson
Owner/Bridal Stylist
Facchianos Bridal and Formal Attire

"I had the pleasure of working Mr. Clark in 2010 when I managed over 2.2 million square feet of downtown office and retail space. I can recommend him highly and without reservation. I had hired Mr. Clark to rebrand the portfolio, and to reach out to prospective tenants.

Throughout the course of the campaign, Mr. Clark was a consummate professional. He conducted market research, built a web-site, and coordinated obtaining pictures, print materials, and gaining media attention within what I would deem a record time. Within the first week of Mr. Clark going public with the campaign, he generated hundreds of prospective tenants.

Mr. Clark's positive attitude is contagious, he is hard worker, and he is genuinely a great guy to work with. I hope that in the near future I will have the opportunity to work with Mr. Clark again."

David Atkinson
One Place, LLC

"Clay, I wanted to thank **you for the incredible seminar I attended on Monday**. I know for sure that it will not only save me lots of money in the near future but make my appliance business profit more than it ever has. Many of my colleagues who attended **were completely wowed by your presentation we could not stop talking about it among ourselves and with others.**

I have already been in contact with a customer who purchased three appliances from me who operates a small sports card shop and also has a radio spot on Saturday mornings with over 10,000 e-mail addresses. I will definitely be in contact with you. Continued success and well wishes for you and your family."

Sincerely
Rick Gallatz
Retail Store Owner

"I have come to realize that foundational sales principles work regardless of what your selling. I work at a coffee shop and my boss told me "Hey, we really need to sell more coffee beans." So I started employing the creative use of imagery, humor, phrasing and tried and true sales methods taught to me by Clay Clark and the book he recommended I read, "Soft Selling In Hard World." I made posters describing the different coffees with funny pop culture references along with legitimate consumer reviews of each coffee. I also began using designing "The 90 second close." Our store shot up to the spot of #1 in whole bean sales out of 613 stores in our entire region. Not only that, but we are averaging 5 pounds sold out of every 1 hundred customers that come into the store where as the average store in the US is averaging 1 to 1.5 pounds per every hundred customers that come in. These numbers don't lie and they just point to the fact that a proper training in sales by someone who knows what they are doing and that has a track record to prove it can make you succeed in sales in whatever business realm you find yourself in, even the coffee shop business."

Scott T.
Store Barista
Starbucks Coffee

"I just wanted to let you know that I took your advice and have, for the past twelve months, been working in the fitness Industry. I finished up my degree (Sports and Health Sciences) and am certified through the National Academy of Sports Medicine. I have officially become the real deal. I am working with ABC on the development of a *Biggest Loser* web series and things are looking up. I just wanted to say thanks for the honest words and tough love when it counted. I still have a long way to go and will keep you posted. I'm excited to see the progress that you have made as well. I'm by no means an Entertainment Legend, but I'm bringing a lot of communication and presentational skills to the table that most people in my industry don't have. Skills that I wouldn't have had it not been for my relationship with *You*! BTW...You are among the most life altering individuals I've ever crossed paths with."

Sincerely
Bucky Brown
Tyler, Texas

"Inspiring, funny, and brilliant! Clay, thank you so much for the brilliant presentations you made to our students in the Spears School of Business at Oklahoma State University. You motivated, entertained, and educated us! We truly appreciate your time and hope to see you again in the near future."

Professor Jeretta Nord
Oklahoma State University, Spears Business School

"Clay, it is seldom that someone inspires me...It is seldom that I am moved by another's attitude and conviction that I take inventory of my own life and make steps toward change. Thank you for encouraging that I read *The Laws of Success*. I ordered it!"

Paige P.
Conference Attendee
Farmers Insurance Agent

"Every day I run this business, I appreciate the level of insight and knowledge of business and systems you brought to the table. Thanks for everything."

TJ Markland
President
Mosaic Productions

"I began working with Clay Clark in 2005. He has helped me develop my internet marketing business to what it is today, teaching me to build sales and delivery systems and goal setting to the point that I now work with multimillion dollar companies like SLAP Watch and ZanyBandz. I would recommend Clay's services to anyone wanting to build the ultimate sales machine."

To Your Success,
Clarence Fisher
Tulsa IM™

"Clay, thank you again for presenting yesterday, I had guests tell me it was the best one of 2011! I know I definitely got some good takeaways for my small business clients. I hope we can have you in again sometime and that you made some good contacts. Have a great day."

Sincerely,
Warren Unsicker
Small Business Program Manager
Tulsa Metro Chamber

"Clay Clark has been instrumental throughout in providing me with the business guidance at the right times!

I have a big vision in what God has called me to do and sometimes as an Entrepreneur you can dream so big that you can lose focus. With three successful companies I knew that it was time for growth and sustainability so that we could reach the people that we needed to reach. I truly believe that God brings certain people into your life at certain times and I thank God for bringing Clay at a time of need. Clay has been instrumental in combining his business savvy with my big vision. The bottomline is that I am in business to help people...but to not run a business but to make money doing it, and that is what Clay has helped me do! If you are considering bringing Clay on for anything business related, it will be the best investment you'll ever make."

Sincerely,
Jonathan Conneely
"Coach JC"
Founder / President, JJC Enterprises
www.CoachJC.com

"We are so happy to have engaged Clay Clark's services for the recent Builder's Convention I recently organized. His ability to meld his presentation in with the specifics of our builder's needs was most impressive. His goal of having each person in that room walk away with one or two items they could implement to help grow their businesses was fully achieved. I would definitely recommend him to anyone looking for an inspiring, motivating speaker to address their group. In fact, we hope to further utilize his additional services addressing specific needs (such as learning to design your website so that it becomes #1 in Google Searches) in the near future. Thank you so much for a wonderful, exciting presentation that brought solid ideas and useful techniques to our group."

Gail M. Stojak
IAUF Executive Asst.
UBuildIt – Orland Park

"Talk about a fun. Our members could not stop talking about how much fun you made the night. You did a great job and we really appreciated it. I have looked into the *SW Nuts* book, I just have not made it over to Barnes and Noble. Again, thanks for doing a great job."

Brad Harris
Harris Pattern & Mfg., Inc.

"Hello Clay, I wanted to personally thank you for your time and talent this last weekend and I have been utilizing the six step sales process and have enjoyed it very much. My personal sales have been affected in the positive. Thank You. Can you by chance give me a list of other books that you recommend? I love the book *Think and Grow Rich*."

Marty
J David Jewelry

"I highly recommend Mr. Clay Clark for his speaking and entertainment services. Clay was the guest speaker at our Student Council District Convention in April 2009 and he was very professional and captivating to the audience. We had 700-plus Middle and High school students and seventy-two teachers in attendance at our convention and Mr. Clark kept these kids and adults entertained the entire time. He not only gave a wonderful speech but he also announced our Talent Show at our convention. We had thirteen schools participating in the talent show and Clay did an awesome job in announcing the acts and getting the audience involved in the show. Clay has a wonderful sense of humor and kept the kids laughing and made our convention a true success. After the convention, I had so many teachers come up to me and say how much they enjoyed the speech and what a wonderful job Clay did in keeping the kids on track and focused during the course of the day with his quick wit and sense of humor. Clay came a little early and stayed a little afterwards and was able to visit and connect with the kids and other teachers on a personal basis to get a feel for his audience. Thanks again for making our convention the success that it was!

Rebecca White
Sponsor of Student Council,
LaGrange High School

"Mr. Clark, I wanted to thank you for speaking to us at the Inspire Conference, your words really meant a lot to me and made me think about things in a whole new light. Thank you again!"

Bianca Hollins
Inspire Conference Attendee,
Oklahoma State University

"Dear Clay, I appreciate all the time you took to talk to us and motivate us. My name is Marisa Drones and I am an Empower student at Rose State College. When you first came in I have to admit I was not sure what you were going to say...But as soon as you started talking I knew I would be changed by the words you spoke! Every saying you gave us, some quoted by others and some your own, truly inspired me. I was not just listening to you, I was *Hearing* you. Thank you for making me want different things in my life and forever changing it! Don't ever quit speaking!"

Sincerely, Marisa Drones Empower Conference Attendee

"My father-in-law just went to a Brand Source National Convention and Summit in Texas and attended a talk you gave. I really learned *A Lot*. You got my mind swirling with ideas so fast I almost couldn't keep up with myself. I would like to read your book and apply your teachings to our business. Thanks again!"

Chuck P.
Sleep Doctor Mattress Gallery

"Thank you for speaking at the Rotaract Club today. You are an inspiration and a wonderful mentor!"

Jeri Barrientos, MBA, AAMS
First Mate Financial Advisors, LLC

"Clay's training has made a *Huge Impact* on my sales team. From cold calling, to closing the deal now. His workshop *Delivers*."

John Toole
Regional Insurance Office Trainer

"No one has ever been so free with information and suggestions as you were...Most folks, like I probably would be, would save that for the paying customers. You gave more good information than I might have ever received (from reading other books and attending numerous other seminars)."

Chad H.
Owner/Operator
UBuildIt-Bethesda

"It is indeed a privilege to recommend Clay Clark to you. Having been in the classroom for over twenty-two years, I have had the opportunity to observe a variety of speakers and others working with my students. None have had the charisma or the ability to capture an audience and engage them as Clay has done. I never miss a chance to have him in my classroom.

He inspires students to be entrepreneurs and challenges them in several areas and to think about their futures. My students always look forward to Clay's visits.

It is difficult to find words to properly describe Clay. He is a unique individual. He is inspiring and entertaining. He is a giver. It has been my experience, once you meet him, you feel like he is your friend. He has qualities that are rarely seen.

Even though Clay's accomplishments speak for themselves, I can honestly say—he is amazing, I have watched him work with some of my most 'challenging' students who were otherwise non-functioning in the classroom and motivate them. He can also relate to the more intelligent as well. Perhaps it is because he is very well read and resourceful that gives him the ability to read his audiences and relate to them. He has experienced success but has also experienced struggles to success—which seems to aid his ability to identify with and engage any audience.

Because of his business experience, insight and ability to work with young people, we have asked Clay to be part of our Advisory Committee for our Family, Career, and Community Leaders of America youth organization at school. Even though he has an extremely full schedule, he has graciously served on this committee for approximately the last four years.

Clay's initiative and level of commitment set him apart from others. He gives more than 100% to whatever he does. I recommend Clay to you with absolute confidence that you will not be disappointed. Feel free to contact me if I can be of assistance."

Sincerely,

Kathy Farquhar, Instructor
Adult & Family Living
FCCLA Advisor
Broken Arrow Senior High School

"10! 10! 10! Clay's presentations were very professional and, yet, humorous. Clay held everyone's attention during both sessions he gave. The time for his sessions seemed to fly by! The information was new and informative to me. I liked the tips Clay pointed out for recognizing opportunities for advancement."

Stacie T. Last
Advanced Audit Techniques Specialist
U.S. Department of Health & Human Services

"We had a lot of compliments about you. In fact one very sweet high school girl sent a thank-you note about you, that when I get a copy of it, I will forward it to you. Hope you know that I appreciate you helping me out this year, and I feel you made a great impact. Thanks a million, Clay!!!"

Deb Ward
RCIDA Project Coordinator

"Clay, we have been hearing rave reviews from our guests about you! Thank you for working with us. Everyone loved you."

Rhonda Anderson
Personal Assistant to the President
ABC Table Top Advertising

"Great flexibility substituting for another speaker. Good job. The "winning @ work" got highest marks from 44 of 56 survey respondents."

John T.
Senior Analyst
U.S. Government Accountability Office

"Clay! I really wanted to thank you for coming down there. I appreciate the time and effort that you put into this trip. The event really got our team *Fired-Up* with *Practical Action Steps*. I have already noted a boost in morale in the office with sales and office personnel referring to things that you said during the meeting. On behalf of V.H. Marketing Ltd. staff, we appreciated your seminar last Saturday. We thank you for coming and enlightening us with your views and thoughts. Please feel free to use me as a reference anytime."

Regards,
Keegan H.
V.H. Marketing Ltd.
Trinidad, West Indies

"I wanted to tell you that you did an awesome job yesterday. I love seeing people hang around after events, such as your workshop, discussing what was just learned and of the ideas they have. I know you have made a difference to those of us that were able to attend (especially for Krista). I hope you will continue your relationship with our SIFE team for years to come. We will be sending you a copy of what we were able to videotape and a copy of the photos taken throughout the workshop and the luncheon. I look forward to conversing with you in the future. Feel free to pass on any ideas you may have for us or for me personally at any time. I would love to keep you as a mentor, as you know we could all use one. Thank You!"

Terri Dubay
Rogers State University SIFE 'Entrepreneurship Day' Organizer

Preface:

"When I grew older and gained insight, I felt that Dad's problem stemmed from the fact that he could not or was not willing to pay the price of ambition. And that responsibility does exact its price." - Stuart Evey (The highest-ranking executive with Getty Oil Company for twenty-six years; the man who directed the launch and development of the sports cable television network E.S.P.N.).

This book is written for the doers not the intenders. The words in this book have the power to transform your life only if you are willing to transform these ideas into action steps. I am writing this book for those rare people who actually take action to solve their problems. I am writing this book for the people out there who are struggling and working hard to unlock the great treasure chest we call wealth. I am writing this for the people who have found the treasure chest, and now all they need is the "magic key" that will let them in. All they need is the "right combination" to unlock these great fortunes.

I am writing this book so the doers, the drivers, and the hard workers out there will have a Step-By-Step ultra-practical guide that will teach the specific action steps one must take to start and grow a successful business. If you *Take Action* and do everything this book tells you to do, you will make millions. If just intend on doing everything in this book, you will make a mediocre living or you will be poor and it will be your own fault.

"Action is the real measure of intelligence." - Napoleon Hill (Apprentice of Andrew Carnegie, Speech Writer for FDR and Author of the *Think & Grow Rich*, the Best-Selling Self-Help Book of all-time.)

Dedication:

This book is dedicated to people whose words and deeds have helped me get to where I now am. Their names appear in the order of which they helped me:

Mom and my Dad, the lady who taught me how to not stutter anymore, Ms. Wilson, Uncle Jerry, Mrs. Jensen, Amanda (my college teacher who helped me the most), Mark DePetris, my beautiful, age-defying wife (Vanessa), Jeremy Thorn, Lori Montag, Napoleon Hill, Shane Harwell, Robert Kiyosaki, Ron Hood, Heath Dean, Clynt Taylor, Rich DePetris, Joel Reyes, Clifton Taulbert, Chet Cadieux, Jack Welch, John Maxwell, Brent Lollis, Michael Gerber, Herb Keller, Jason Bailey, Braxton Fears, Jerry Vass, Donald Trump, Jonathan Barnett, Jonathan Conneely, and my five beautiful kids.

WHEEL OF WEALTH

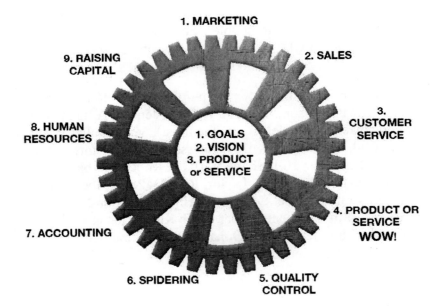

1. MARKETING

9. RAISING
CAPITAL

2. SALES

8. HUMAN
RESOURCES

1. GOALS
2. VISION
3. PRODUCT
or SERVICE

3.
CUSTOMER
SERVICE

7. ACCOUNTING

4. PRODUCT OR
SERVICE
WOW!

6. SPIDERING

5. QUALITY
CONTROL

Table of Contents:

******

Who Is Clay Clark and Why Is He Qualified To Tell Me What To Do?

"I am America's most humble man." - Clay Clark

Y ou shouldn't spend your time listening to the advice of people who have never done what you want to do. You should never get fitness tips from an over-weight trainer, business tips from your broke Uncle Jim, or marital tips from someone who has been divorced three times. If you think like a successful entrepreneur and do what a successful entrepreneur does wouldn't you become successful? If you only get your advice from some college professor or academic who has never achieved business or financial success, isn't it likely that you will never achieve success as well? My friend you need to listen to a successful entrepreneur. I am not qualified to give you fitness tips or advice on how to improve your golf swing, but I was the "United States Small Business Administration Entrepreneur of the Year" because I know how to start and grow businesses. Over the years, I've started numerous successful businesses and organizations of my own. During this time, I've also been blessed with the opportunity to successfully coach nearly every type of business imaginable including: appliance stores, attorneys, auto detailers, bakeries, basketball coaches, bootcamp fitness programs, churches, coffee shops, commercial real estate professionals, cupcake businesses, disk jockey companies, event planners, financial planners, hair salons, health insurance providers, hotels, ID manufacturers, internet marketers, insurance companies, jewelers, landscapers, leadership experts, medical product resellers, ministries, mortgage companies, motivational speakers, multi-level marketers, paint suppliers, photographers, purse manufacturers, real estate companies, restaurants, snow cone shop owners, staffing companies, supplement manufacturers, travel planners, universities, web developers, videographers, women's groups, nothing that starts with an "x", and the Zenith awards. As I've traveled around the country helping these people and organizations, I've discovered that the process of achieving success in any type of business is very similar. If you go down the wrong path, bad things happen. If you implement the "best practice" business strategies that have been proven to work time and time again, you will succeed. It doesn't matter how many hours you pour into your website updates or how many sales calls you make if you are doing it the wrong way. It doesn't matter how hard you work or how smart you are if you don't have the right keys. If you don't know the specific action steps you need to take to unlock your true prosperity, it will never happen. There is a strong chance that everyone reading this is smarter than me. I took my ACT multiple times to get into college and I probably would have never passed if it wasn't for the specific strategies I learned from a course I purchased. Throughout the course of this book, I will teach you the specific strategies and action steps you need to take to unlock your true potential and to pass the test of entrepreneurship.

My Story:

I grew up in a middle-class family in Oklahoma, and then I moved with our family up to Minnesota so my parents could find sustainable work while moving closer to family. At age sixteen, I started a D.J. service and T-shirt business using money I had earned working on a farm. I took my A.C.T. three times to get into college at Oral Roberts University. I grew the D.J. service out of my dorm room into the nation's largest (non-franchised) wedding entertainment company (DJConnectionTulsa.com). When I was twenty, I was named the Metro Chamber of Commerce, "Young Entrepreneur of the Year." I started the Tulsa Bridal Association with Lori Montag (the founder of Zany Bandz & Slap Watch). Lori and I started the Tulsa Bridal Association Wedding Show. Since 2003, I have started or partnered with eleven different companies ranging from commercial real estate, and insurance to bakeries and sports fitness related companies. In 2007, I was named the United States Small Business Administration's "Entrepreneur of the Year."

Today, I coach with countless entrepreneurs and business owners around the country helping them achieve their business goals while running my businesses. I limit my speaking events to four per month, because I have five incredible kids and one incredible wife who I don't want to be apart from too often. I wouldn't have achieved success without the incredible mentorship of the people mentioned earlier and without my insatiable appetite to learn more. This book is designed to help you achieve what I have achieved while helping you to avoid some of the growing pains that I went through because I simply did not know what to do most of the time. This book is designed to save you the time needed to read everything I've read, and all of the mentorship I needed to have. This book is designed to help you *Get Rich Quicker*.

******

An Overview:
What Is the Wheel of Wealth?
If it is not scalable and duplicatable it is not
worth doing or it is a hobby.

A t the core, nearly every successful business is the same. And at the end of the day, every business exists to build wealth for its owner by providing a solution for problems that people have. If you want to become rich you have to find a *Big Problem* and then you have to *Solve It* over and over again. People had a problem. They wanted to get from A to B quickly for business or personal travel without losing their bags, without arriving late, without being charged huge prices, without encountering hidden fees, and without the hassle of unfriendly employees. Southwest Airlines solved this problem. That is why Southwest Airlines has made many people wealthy. People had a problem. They wanted to enjoy coffee in environment that felt like home, but that was not home. They wanted a place where they could enjoy a cup of coffee with their business associates and friends that felt classy and comfortable. People wanted to enjoy coffee that didn't have floating chunks of burnt coffee floating in it. People wanted to enjoy premium coffee in a premium environment. Starbucks solved this problem. That is why Starbucks Coffee has made many people wealthy. What problems are people still having? How will you become wealthy by solving these problems?

Before you get a loan, before you spend your hard earned money on tuition studying entrepreneurship, before you lease space, before you spend a dime and before you spend your precious time, you must be able to answer these eight questions:

1. What is a problem people have?

---

2. What solutions can I provide for these problems?

---

3. How much will people be willing to pay for the solutions I provide?

---

4. Is my solution duplicatable and scalable?

---

5. What are my ideal lifestyle goals?

---

6. How much money annually will it cost me to live my ideal lifestyle? _____

7. How many problems will I have to solve in order to afford to live my ideal lifestyle?

---

8. Is it possible to live my ideal lifestyle by solving this problem with my solutions?

If the answer to Question 8 is 'No,' then you need to come up with a different problem to solve. Don't spend your hard earned money and the precious few hours you have on the planet solving problems for people if solving these problems doesn't have the potential to make you wealthy.

It costs money to live your ideal lifestyle. It costs profound amounts of money to fund all the charities you like, to feed all the kids you have (or will have), to buy all the houses, cars, and boats you want to have, to go on vacation when you want and to buy that really cool cowboy that your four year-old son "needs" to have. Those "American Girl" dolls are expensive. Don't sell yourself short. Don't waste your time on this planet starting a business that is a *Waste of Your Time*.

Assuming that your answer to Question 8 is 'Yes,' then it's time for you to get to work. Starting a successful business is not tricky. Starting a successful business does not require above average intelligence. Starting a successful business **does require having a <u>pig-headed, purpose-driven tenacity</u> about achieving your life goals and fulfilling your life's vision through providing products and services that offer uncompromising quality in a <u>scalable and duplicatable way</u>.**

As you read this incredibly-humble, practical, and ultra-action orientated entrepreneurship guide-book, I will walk you through the "Wheel of Wealth" and the eight areas of every successful business. If you master these nine areas, you will become wealthy. If you can't master these nine areas, find a partner who can help you master some of the parts that you aren't good at, or hire a business coach who can help you through this process. This should excite you! You only have nine core areas to master en route to earning your riches, so that you can begin living a more abundant life. And worst case scenario, if you don't master these nine core areas you can go back to having small dreams, living in a small house, going on small vacations and helping people who have small needs.

My friend, mentally marinate on the profoundness of this. *If You Master These Nine Areas, You Will Be Rich.* What would that feel like? No more coupons. No more looking-around for good deals all the time. No more delaying maintenance on your car to afford the payment. No more life without AC in your apartment. No more years without vacations. No more inability to pay your bills. My friend, I once lived without AC during Tulsa, Oklahoma's hot summers, I've been there too! It is not fun, but I am telling you from personal experience. *You Can Do This. Master These Eight Areas And You Will Make Big Money!* Let's get started!

*****

Profound Truth 1: The Center of the Wheel

The intangible passion that makes everything else possible.

"Where there is no vision, the people perish." - Proverbs 29:18

If you don't have clearly written out goals, a vision for your life and the openness to develop the products or services with which you can use to create the wealth needed to fund your life then the rest of this book is not necessary. If you don't have your goals written down, you will never achieve them for the same reason a truck driver will never get his load to a given location if he doesn't know what city he is going to. This might sound like a simple concept, yet study after study shows that *Most People Do Not Have Their Goals Written Down.* Weird! This is nuts to me! How do you and I ever expect to get something if we don't even know what we want? If a genie told most people that he would grant their wish immediately, most people wouldn't even know what they want out of life. What do you want out of life? What is the vision what you have for your life? What do you want to achieve? If you could write your own eulogy in advance, what would you want it to say? My friend, I have helped numerous people to build successful businesses. I have coached with Fortune 500 companies. I have helped firms both large and small to make more money, but I can't create something from nothing. You must know the answer to these questions, or you are beyond help:

1) What are your five-year goals?

_____

_____

_____

_____

_____

_____

_____

2) What is the overall vision you have for your life (what is your ideal lifestyle)?

_____

_____

_____

_____

_____

_____

_____

If you want to turn your passion into profits, I can show you how to do that. If you want to make profits so that you can have enough money to pursue your passions, I can show you how to do that too. If you want to know the real secrets to weight loss success, I cannot help you. My friend, let's get busy. We can sleep when we're dead.

*****

Profound Truth 2: The Power of Imagination, Determination & Tenacity

In order to succeed in business and life, you need IQ, EQ, and AQ.

- **IQ (Intelligence Quotient)** - Everyone knows about IQ, the intelligence quotient that academics love to talk about. Unfortunately, IQ is only a score derived from different standardized tests designed to gauge your level of intelligence relative to your age. Essentially IQ only measures potential. If IQ was the big factor that determined one's overall level of success, Henry Ford would have been homeless, I would be living with my mother, and everyone on 'Jeopardy' would be leading Forbes' list of America's wealthiest individuals every year.

- **EQ (Emotional Quotient)** - Very few academics know about the emotional quotient or event talk about the emotional quotient, because this is something that people can control. Essentially, your EQ measures your overall ability to rebound emotionally from tough situations. Nearly all of America's wealthiest individuals score unbelievably high in this area. Bill Belichick, the legendary coach of the New England Patriots, has an unbelievable EQ. This guy was told by every coach in high school that he did not have what it took to play in high school or college. Undeterred, he transmuted his love of the game into an intense focus for watching game film and coaching. During high school he became the guru of game film and football coaching systems. How many kids would have just given up on their football career aspirations after being told point blank that they didn't have the skills or talents needed to succeed in football? Bill's high EQ allowed him to focus on being the best high school coach's assistant and team manager possible. His high EQ has turned him into one of professional sports' most consistent winners of all time.

- **AQ (Attitudinal Quotient)** - Almost nobody on the planet has a high AQ. Those that do win. Those that do not must settle for mediocrity. Your AQ measures your ability to maintain an optimal attitude regardless of the circumstances around you. It's easy to have a great attitude when everything is working. But what about when things fall apart? When things fall apart, most people and aspiring entrepreneurs begin to scale back their dreams. They begin to dream "safe dreams" to avoid the risk of failure. To achieve and succeed on the planet Earth, you must have a high AQ. When Prime Minister Winston Churchill famously stood up to Hitler and his fascist regime, he stood alone. Without the support of the United States, who was reluctant to get into a war with the powerful Nazis, he famously stood up and spoke to the British people, "We have before us an ordeal of the most grievous kind. We have before us many, many long months of struggle and of suffering. You ask what is our policy? I will say: It is to wage war, by sea, land, and air, with all our might and with all the strength that God can give us; to wage war against a monstrous tyranny, never surpassed in the dark, lamentable catalogue of human crime. That is our policy. You ask, what is our aim? I answer in one word: Victory. Victory at all costs! Victory in spite of all terror, victory however long and hard the road may be; for without victory, there is no survival." It is simply impossible to succeed without a high AQ.

At the end of the day, your level of success is going to be determined by the **power of your imagination, the level of your determination, the intensity of your tenacity.** Every week I get a call from someone that has a *"Big Idea."* The caller always has this incredible idea that is going to *"Change The Way People Do This or That."* And initially I am excited for the person I am talking to. However, after asking them just two or three questions, my enthusiasm quickly transforms into near cynicism as they provide me with an endless list of reasons, excuses, and alibis as to why their product has not taken off yet. In no particular order, here are the most common excuses I hear from those unwilling to take responsibility for their lives.

- *"I want to sell my product nationwide, but you have to be well known before retailers will even talk to you."*

- *"I feel like I'm on the verge of something big, but my employees just don't seem motivated."*

- *"I know this idea will be huge, but I just don't have the capital I need!"*

- *"My business was going great and then we lost one of our key employees and he stole all the business from us."*

- *"You don't understand my business, it's just not scalable like yours."*

- *"This line of work is different; I just can't train people quickly like you do."*

- *"I want to make a schedule for myself, but I have to pick my kids up this Thursday...and then next Tuesday I* *have a game, and then Saturdays are tough because of the divorce, and...(**I Vomit Right Around Here**)."*

- *"To me I would rather have a good family than a bunch of money. Right now I'm just focusing on my family.*

- *"In my line of work it's really hard to hold people accountable because we are just too spread out."*

- *"My business just can't grow because I can't find the right people."*

- *"I just don't have the accounting systems I need to watch expenses like I am supposed to."*

- *"Right now, we are wanting to grow, but with the economy being how it is, I just think we are going to have to wait it out until it turns around."*

- *"I have been trying to get the Performa and business strategy created, but I just had a long weekend."*

- *"I'm just not a reader. I know I should be, but I just don't have the time."*

- *"I'm just not good at cold calling. I prefer to meet people face to face."*

- *"I feel like my customers want more of a personalized service, so I don't want to get Big, yet. I don't want to grow too fast."*

- *"My fiancé (girlfriend, boyfriend, husband, wife, or uncle), thinks this might just not be a good idea right now."*

- *"It's really hard for me to know my schedule with our type of business."*

If you are not careful and if you say these excuses enough times you will begin to believe them. And if you have an IQ that is just high enough, you will actually be able begin using these excuses as "valid justifications" for your mediocrity. Smart people can justify anything. Most people can come up with tons of excuses for their mediocrity. But you are not most people because you have decided that you are going to be a success. Go ahead and say it out loud! Thoughts become words. Words become actions. Actions become habits. Habits become our reputation. Our reputations determine how high we can climb on the success ladder. To go ahead and start creating your own momentum by declaring out loud, YOU ARE GOING TO BECOME A SUCCESS! Success is not normal. Success is not common. But you have decided to become uncommon. You have decided to take the action steps needed to become exceptional! You have decided to accept responsibility for where you currently are in life. You have decided to take ownership of your own results. Unlike most people you realize that the *Law of Cause & Affect* affects us all whether we acknowledge it or not.

The story goes that once upon a time the great mind Albert Einstein was asked a question by a Mom about how to raise a child to become a genius? He responded by saying, "Read the child more fairy tales." Essentially, people without imagination and a *Big Idea* have no hope of ever succeeding beyond mediocrity in life. However, the Mom did not ask Albert Einstein how to teach a genius to become successful? The path the success involves two parts. Part One is all about imagination and dreaming up a big idea. Part Two is all about having the diligence, the determination, and the tenacity needed to turn those dreams into reality. First comes the inspiration, then comes the perspiration.

Part One: The Power of Imagination

The famous author, L. Frank Baum, who wrote the classic, *The Wonderful Wizard of Oz*, had one of the most prolific imaginations of all-time. This guy wrote over fifty-five novels and 200 poems during his epic career. In his novels and writings, he wrote about the laptop computer, he wrote about his visions for color televisions and a phone without wires. His imagination had no limits. But, what if he didn't have the determination and the diligence to write it all down? How long does it take to write fifty-five novels and 200 poems? Do you think this guy ever had "writer's block?" Absolutely. Did he ever quit? No. During Walt Disney's famous career, he too had *Big Dreams* and a *Wild Imagination.*

As an ambulance driver, young Walt day-dreamed of becoming an artist. He would doodle on anything he had in front of him and he even went to the extreme of painting his ambulance "to be more appealing for young kids." However, what if he did not have the determination to overcome his first and second failed business ventures? Each time he started his studio, his costs would outrun his income and his businesses would fail. Could you imagine starting two businesses that completely failed? Most people don't have the boldness and the courage needed to start one business, let alone to start another one after having failed.

Henry Ford had the *Bold Idea* of transforming the world with his "assembly line." Because no one had ever witnessed his inventions in their physical reality, many people thought he was crazy. He envisioned machines that people could use to mass-produce an automobile that would be affordable for the masses. He believed this expensive luxury item of its day would eventually become something that whole country could enjoy. However, what if he had quit after he went broke the first time? He could have justified it. What if he would have quit after he lost it all the second time? He could have given his friends a valid excuse for his failure. What if he quit after the third or fourth times? I'm sure his friends would have patted him on the back and told him some ridiculous false kindness like, "Hey Henry, at least you did your best. You know maybe it just wasn't mean to be?" Maybe a spiritual friend would have said, "Henry, sometimes God has to shut a door before he opens another one up?" To quote the incredibly deep American classic film, *Dumb & Dumber*, he would have been known as "one pathetic loser" if he had not have gotten himself off the ground. If he had not been able to motivate himself to start again, Henry Ford would have been unknown to us today, because he would have been a failure in business.

Remember Super Bowl Champ and Dallas Cowboys' coach Jimmy Johnson? Remember his hair? He had the big idea that he could team up with his college buddy Jerry Jones to reignite the passion and the success of America's team. He started out 1-15 in 1989. And 1990 wasn't much better. He then went on to win multiple Super Bowls with the Dallas Cowboys. Hall of Fame Coach Chuck Noll believed that he could turn the Steelers into champions, he started out 1-13 in 1969 before later going to become known as one of the greatest football coaches of all-time. The mastermind behind the San Francisco 49ers football dynasty and the designer of the famous "West Coast Offense" Bill Walsh started his first year out 2-14 in 1979. What if these men didn't have the guts and the tenacity to believe in their systems?

Part Two: Determination & Tenacity

Determination and tenacity are the things that keep us hammering away when our hands get sore and our arms get tired. Determination is that thing that actually causes us to increase our resolve with each rejection. Determination is that degree of separation that makes people winners or losers. Whether you are opening up a salon, starting a wedding entertainment company or building an insurance office, success is not possible without determination.

Do you get reinvigorated, stirred up, and more motivated by each rejection or do you have only enough determination to put your system in place until you experience some setbacks during your first year? Would you know who Walt Disney was if he had quit after going broke the first time? Would it completely, rock your brain to know that Walt Disney actually lost it all twice before becoming a "success."

Did you know that success is absolutely unavoidable when a person has a *Great Big Idea,* a proven game plan and the *Will to Never Quit?* Did you know that Coca Cola only sold 400 cokes during its first year? Did you know that President George Washington was getting slaughtered by the British troops before he decided to completely reformulate his strategy of fighting against the British? Do you remember when Apple Computers was the laughing stock of every high school computer lab? No one wanted Apple computers. People mocked them and they had such a small percentage of the market. Success seemed impossible to almost everyone, except for Steve Jobs. Did you know that Conrad Hilton started a bank that failed? Did you know Mr. Hilton ran out of cash during the depression and actually came within $25,000 of bankruptcy? Did you know he asked everyone he knew for the money and the only person who came to his aid was his mother? Have you asked your mother for $25,000? Have you asked everyone you know? Have you called every lead? Have you actually gotten back up after being knocked down? Have you raised your AQ and EQ to the level needed to achieve success. My father always told me, "In the game of football it is not a question about whether you will get hurt or not. It's a question about how many times you are going to get hurt and how bad you are going to get hurt." Business is the same way. If you aren't prepared to spend some time rehabbing from an injury every once in a while you shouldn't start a business, and you should reduce the size of your dreams immediately so you can quit wasting your time.

Harvey Mackay, who is a fabulous author and successful business person wrote, "Be like a postage stamp. Stick to it until you get there." This phrase is absolutely what it is all about. So how does this apply to you and your business?

- How big of a vision do you have for your life? Do you dream safe dreams so that you won't have to deal with rejection? What would Steve Jobs have done?

- How tenacious are you being about your prospecting? Do you quit after seventy-five calls to run home early because you are frustrated? What would Conrad Hilton have done?

- How determined are you being about your systems? Do you quit when the first, second, third, or fourth hourly employee won't follow them? What would Walt Disney have done? Would he have lowered his expectations to meet the demands of an outspoken and mediocre employee? Would he have lowered his expectations for his life and his "Magic Kingdom" simply because some poor family member in his family told him that "you might want to have a backup plan in case this thing doesn't work?"

- In what areas of your life are you dreaming small?

- In what areas of your business are you showing feeble amounts of determination?

It's a good thing that IQ is not the main variable that determines someone's success or failure. As stated, if that was the case I would be living under a bridge banging on buckets for money. The level of your EQ and the level of your AQ are what matters and it is something that you can control. You will achieve success, I have achieved success and my clients have achieved success because they had a big imagination and the determination and tenacity needed to turn these "*Big Ideas*" into "*Big Results*."

*****

Profound Truth 3: Momentum

How to create it and why it will never come if you wait for it.

"Create a definite plan for carrying out your desire and begin at once, whether you ready or not, to put this plan into action."
- Napoleon Hill

In order to get your "Wheel of Wealth" moving you are going to have to create some momentum in your life. You must get in the habit of doing, instead of talking. You must get in the habit of completing and seeing things through rather than just intending to do things. You are going to have to come to grips with the fact that you are where you are right in life because of the things you have done or have failed to do. Every high school guidance counselor in America tells every kid in America that they have "potential." They love this word. To me the word "potential" means a list of stuff that I've talked about doing, but haven't done yet.

That might sound harsh, but my friend, the world judges us not based on what we intended to do but based on what we have actually done. Could you imagine the hit show, *The Biggest Loser*, giving away the prize to person who intended on losing the most weight? Could you imagine what would happen if the bank allowed us to fill out and deposit the money that we "might make in the future"? Could you imagine how our country would quickly fall apart if we all got paid based on what we intended on doing, rather than what we actually did?

In order for you to be successful you are going to have to become great at *quickly* turning the ideas the come into your head into tangible to do lists and action steps. You then need to become great at completing those to-do lists with a sense of urgency.

Successful people think like this:

1. Study successful people and businesses to stimulate new ideas.

2. Think of new ideas.

3. Write down new ideas.

4. Make the "to-do list" needed to turn new ideas into realities.

5. Schedule *specific times* to complete "to-do-lists" items.

6. Deposit *results* into the bank account.

Unsuccessful people think like this.

1. Hang around negative and unsuccessful people and watch successful people on TV and in magazines.

2. Wish for things and occasionally think of new ideas.

3. Habitually forget to write things down.

4. Occasionally make "to-do lists," but rarely complete them.

5. Never schedule *specific times* to accomplish anything. Always say, "I don't have enough time to _____?"

6. Try to convince the bank teller to let you deposit your "intentions" into the bank account, when your results are poor.

In order to become a successful person you will need to keep the following items with you at all times:

1. A "To-Do List" - You can't achieve success, if you don't know what specific action steps you must take today in order to get there. Typically my "To-Do Lists" are three pages long and they are sorted in order of importance. There is absolutely no

way to be successful if you don't write down your ideas, and the action steps needed to achieve them.

2. A "Day-Timer" - You must learn to schedule *Specific* times to turn your "To-Do Lists" into reality. We are all busy, and you must become a *Time-Management Expert* if you are going to achieve success. What time will you start the project? In order to add something (money, etc....) into your life, you must become comfortable with taking something out of your life. Look at your day timer and make the tough decisions now. What time wasters are in your schedule? Take the steps neede to eliminate as many of these time wasting activities now.

"Cherish your visions and your dreams as they are the children of your soul, the blueprints of your ultimate achievements." - Napoleon Hill

*****

Profound Truth 4: What is entrepreneurship?

Why the world always needs another problem solver.

"Entrepreneurs solve the world's problems and unapologetically make money doing it." - Clay Clark (United States Small Business Administration Entrepreneur of the Year)

Bottom line, entrepreneurs solve problems for people and then they charge for their solutions. If your business idea does not solve problems for people in a compelling way, it is not going to work.

Problem 1: People need natural gas for their homes.

Solution 1: Helmrich & Payne - The Company that came up with the best way to drill horizontally to find gas that was previously not available can now charge natural gas companies for their solution.

Problem 2: People want to be entertained at wedding receptions, and they have a budget of $1,000.

Solution 2: DJ Connection - The Company that can consistently deliver the most fun entertainment and the most helpful and entertaining customer service system will make the most money.

Problem 3: People want to know how to start a business *now*, and they don't want to sit in a classroom for four years entrepreneurship tips from a professor who has never started a business before.

Solution 3: This book - The book than can teach you the *Specific Action Steps You Need to Take* to start or a grow a successful business quickly.

Problem 4: You aren't exactly sure what problem you are going to solve for the world.

Solution 4: Write down fifty (I like that number) problems that you experienced this week, and a service / product that could solve those problems.

Problem 5: You have an existing business that is not making enough money.

Solution 5: Write down fifty problems that your business could solve for your existing customers.

**Note: Use the rest of this page to write down problems and solutions. If you can't do this part, stop reading this book, use it as fuel for your fireplace and go get a job working for someone who already solves problems.

******

Profound Truth 5:   Goals

Your business exists to solve problems for you and your customers.

"First comes thought; then organization of that thought, into ideas and plans; then transformation of those plans into reality. The beginning, as you will observe, is in your imagination." - Napoleon Hill (Author of *Think & Grow Rich*)

Your business only exists to solve problems for you and your customers. What are your problems? What are your goals? If money were no object, what would you do with your time? Why can't you just modify your goals to fit within the limitations imposed by not being successful? Why can't you just tone down your ambition a little?

Why won't you just settle for a cubicle job somewhere? There are millions of jobs out there. If you just show up on time every day and do what you are supposed to do you will most surely become a manager quickly. No one shows up on time and does what they are supposed to do anymore. You will be a genius amongst idiots. My friend, you will become a manager *Quickly.* Soon you will get benefits, health insurance and "paid time off!" Oh yeah! Someday soon you will even get "personal days!" And because of labor unions no one will even be allowed to ask you where you were without violating your rights. What is your problem? Why not just go and work as a cog in a wheel? Why are you so determined to ACHIEVE BIG GOALS with your life?

Why do your goals have to be so big? Your problem is that you want to make BIG MONEY. To ever turn your BIG GOALS into a BIG REALITY you are going to have to make HUGE SUMS OF MONEY. Helping lots of people with your

1

EXTREME FINANCIAL GEROSITY is going to cost you. If you keep on liking granite, leather, BMWs, convertibles, Disney vacations, generous giving, financial independence and completed time freedom you are going to need to be a part owner or a 100% owner of a BIG BUSINESS that solves a lot of problems for a lot of people.

Thus, if you are starting a business that will not allow you to do this, you really need to quit immediately. If you are selling a product or service for $600 and you only have the capacity to sell four of these items per week you need to quit what you are doing a look for another problem to solve. You have to solve huge amount of problems for an enormous amount of people if you are ever going to get rich. Do not let the profoundness of this concept escape you. FROM NOW ON, IF THE BUSINESS YOU ARE THINKING OF STARTING IS NOT SCALABLE & DUPLICATABLE IF DONE RIGHT, THEN YOU MUST STOP WORKING ON THIS BUSINESS PLAN IMMEDIATELY. STOP WORKING ON SMALL AND PATHETIC BUSINESS MODELS. You don't get extra glory in heaven because you started a "local mom and pop shop." If you are going to start a business you must start a business that is designed to go *Big Time* or it is not worth doing for you. Successful entrepreneurs all work over 60 hours per week during the start-up phase and it's going to be tough. If you are going to make *Big Money*, you are going to have to create a *Big Time Business*.

So again I ask you? What is your problem? What are your *Goals*? Why are you such an *Enemy of Average*? Why are you so determined to do big things, with your life? Why won't you just settle?

Questions for you to answer now:

1) How much money do you need to make to afford the lifestyle you want and to achieve the goals you have?

2) How much profit will you make per customer?

3) How many customers will you have to serve to achieve your goals? (What is the specific number?)

4) Is this number feasible? If this number is not, think of another business idea quickly before you lose motivation.

If you need more information on this subject visit: **www.MakeYourLifeEpic.com or give us a call today at 918-851-6920 and we will help you come up with a business idea that will help you achieve your goals.

*****

Profound Truth 6: Luck

How to create your own big breaks.

"I'm a great believer in luck, and I find the harder I work, the more I have of it."

- Thomas Jefferson

If you are ever going to become the kind of person who achieves huge amounts of success, you must learn to focus only on what you can control. You can't control the weather. You can't control the thoughts of other people. You can't control the overall economy. However you can control your thoughts, your expectations and your luck. The thing that most unsuccessful people refer to as "luck" is simply nothing more than the intersection of preparation and opportunity. If you prepare yourself and you are constantly doing the little things right, you will find yourself getting opportunities that never would have happened before. You must be prepared for when these opportunities occur. However, there is a three-part system you must implement to create these opportunities for yourself daily.

- Part 1: Contact people of influence daily

- Part 2: Build a massive database of humans that you have met

- Part 3: Take more shots than anyone else in the game.

Part One: Contact people of influence daily

You must quickly grasp the truth that, "It's not what you know, but who you know." You must begin systematically reaching out to the people of influence that you need to know. If you don't reach out to these people you will never know them. There is a very strong possibility that billionaires, investors, celebrities and successful entrepreneurs are not going to wake up tomorrow with your *Specific Name* in their heads and a *Huge Motivation* to mentor you to back it up.

You must reach out to the people who you need to know to get where you want to go. Every morning you must commit to reaching out to these people. *Every Day* you must do this. Are you going to actually do this or are you going to "try to remember?" You must commit to doing this every day or you will fail and it will be your fault.

Part Two: Build a massive database of humans that you have met

Because you are in that elite group of people that actually do things, instead of just intending to do things, soon you are going to find yourself going out to eat with hotel owners, billionaires, multi-millionaires, celebrities, mayors, and other people of influence. This is great, but merely getting in front of them is not enough.

When you meet these people you must be very intentional about building rapport with them, finding out where they want to go with their lives and how you can help them get there in a way that benefits both of you. Once you determine this information, you must save it into your database so that you can quickly find their information when you need it. You must determine how it is that you will help this person of influence to turn their goals into reality in a way that benefits both of you. You then must take *Action*. Pretty soon you will find yourself in partnership with people of influence. Pretty soon you will find yourself hanging out with the same people. You will soon be sitting at the same tables with these successful people. You will find yourself wearing the same clothes and doing the same things. You will find yourself succeeding.

My friend, birds of a feather flock together. Don't hang out with a bunch of penguins that are incapable of flying. Hang around eagles soaring through the sky with the greatest of ease. Have them teach you how, and pretty soon you too will become an eagle. Once you meet these eagles, you must save their *Name, Number, E-Mail Address, Occupation*, and *Their Goals* into your database. If you need help setting up this database you are not alone. In fact most of the clients that I work with did not have a fully optimized database in place capable of prompting them to contact these individuals in a proactive way before I began working with them. If you need help setting up this system call 918-851-6920 and we will help you out. However, regardless of who helps you, you must maintain contact with these leaders in a systematic, proactive and positive way.

Part Three: Take more shots than anyone else in the game.

You will never be "lucky enough" to hit a game-winning shot if you never actually shoot the ball. In fact your probability of ever hitting a game-winning shot will increase exponentially just by shooting the ball exponentially more. In fact Michael Jordan, who was one of the best professional basketball players of all time, is famous for saying "I've missed more than 9,000 shots in my career. I've lost almost 300 games. Twenty-six times, I've been trusted to take the game winning shot and missed. I've failed over and over and over again in my life. And that is why I succeed."

Thus, the question you need to ask yourself is this. Are you shooting enough? If you can't handle rejection and losing from time to time you will never succeed. This is some *Serious Stuff*

Here. If you can't deal with missing shots in front of a sellout crowd, then you don't have what it takes to achieve greatest, thus you must go to work for someone else as soon as possible or you will be very poor.

*****

Profound Truth 7: Time Management - Time is your most
important asset, manage it wisely.

*"Time is the scarcest resource of the manager; If it is not
managed, nothing else can be managed."* - Peter F. Drucker
(Management Expert, Pioneer and Guru)

I think that spending a lot of time, dwelling on the importance
of time would not be a good use of anyone's time so I will get
right down to the point. Oprah, Bill Gates, Michael Jackson,
Gandhi, Will Smith, Henry Ford, Russell Simmons, Jay-Z, you,
and I all have the same amount of time every day to turn our
lives into a reality. We all have twenty-four hours per day if we
don't get hit by a bus. Thus, I believe that it would make sense
for us all to become time-management experts, because this
really means that we would all be life management experts. In
just a moment, I will show you my daily system. It works, but
it won't work if you don't work. Here it is.

Step 1.

Every day, wake up before everyone else in your home
does.

Create a quiet time for yourself where you just "think and
plan." Henry Ford (the famous automobile Tycoon) once
famously said, "Thinking is the hardest work there is,
which is probably the reason why so few engage in it."
How many of us actually take time out to think and plan
each morning? I do. How about you?

Step 2.

Write down your goals for the following five categories (spirit, mind, body, relationships and finance). Remember to make *Big Daily* goals for yourself.

Donald Trump was right when he said, "If you're going to be thinking anything, you might as well think big." My friend you have to make *Big* daily goals for yourself everyday if you are going to ever create life momentum. Write down the five categories listed above and make a goal in each of these areas that you can achieve every day.

Step 3.

Commit to getting everything on your list done every day.

When you accomplish something you will feel good about yourself. When you cross an item off of your to-do-list you will feel better about yourself. The more you get done, the better you will feel. The better you feel the more confident and ambitious you will feel. You must build life momentum every day. If you are living in your mom's basement waiting for the ladies (or dudes) to call to take you on a hot date, it is not going to happen. You must jump start your own life by getting up early, making a to-do-list and committing to accomplishing it every day!

Step 4.

Only work via appointment.

Don't take random calls when you can afford not to. If you don't have a support staff, just set up blocks of time where you focus on one thing. Focusing on everything all at once will cause your life vision to become blurry and your brain to explode. Trust me on this. I learned this the hard way from first-hand experience. If you wanted to meet with the CEO of any big company, you probably would have to set an appointment. The chances of you just "grabbing him for a few minutes to pick his brain" are very slim. My friend, you must learn to set appointments for everything in your life. Set appointments to work out. Set appointments to make out with your spouse. Set appointments to meet with people. Set appointments to pay bills and hold yourself accountable. To make this happen you must carry a day-timer at all times.

Step 5.

Only engage in mutually beneficial relationships.

If someone cannot benefit you and you cannot benefit them on some level you do not need to waste your life (time) having these bogus interactions and meetings. You must be able to tell people "No". My friend, I had to start charging people for business coaching because I had literally hundreds of "great intenders" and "non-doers-of-anything" calling me see if they could "pick my brain" and "take me out to lunch". They saw my success and wanted it. They saw the 6,000 square foot house on 5 acres and they wanted it. They read my press clippings and they wanted the profits we were making. However, most of these people were just intenders who refused to take action to transform their big ideas into reality. If I can't add value to something I am not going to be on your committee. If you cannot benefit from having a meeting with someone, learn to say "No". Say it graciously, but say it often. Say "No!"

Step 6.

Only focus on what you can control.

If two dudes are talking about their discontentment with politics and the weather do not participate in this conversation. If someone is contemplating the various nuances of the Earth's religions walk away. My friend, only focus on things that you can control. If you have a fixable problem, fix it. If it is not fixable, move on to something that is. I'm white. He's black. She's Asian. He's a dude. She's a lady. He's smarter than I am. She's taller than I am. Who cares? Just focus on what you can control. He came from wealth. She came from poverty. You came from poverty too. Get over it. Your Dad was a jerk. Her Dad was great. Her Mom was there for her and your Mom wasn't. Get over it! You must learn to focus only on what you can control.

Step 7.

Pay experts and charge if you are one.

If you want to save yourself a bunch of time, it is always easier to be a pirate than a pioneer. I'm telling you this from firsthand experience here. For me the few hours I have spent being coached and mentored by Lori Montag (founder of Zany Bandz and Slap Watch), Clifton Taulbert (*New York Times* Best-Selling Author and Entrepreneur), Chet Cadieux (the C.E.O. of QuikTrip Convenience Stores) and David Green (the founder of Hobby Lobby) have completely changed my life. Had I just gone out and "tried my best" I probably would still be struggling in many areas. Why must you go out and reinvent the wheel? If someone knows what you need to know, just pay them for their information and their years of experience. Remember that time is the only asset you can't make more of. Sara Blakely, the founder of the billion dollar Spanx company credits the success coach and millionaire mentor T. Harve Eker for helping her to completely transform her way of thinking so that she could being earning millions. Study successful people and do what they tell you to do. Read their book or pay them for a half hour of their time. Sometimes fifteen minutes with a guru is all you need to get from where you are to where you want to be. If you are a guru, you really need to charge others for your time. If you have people constantly coming to you to ask for your advice, you must charge them or you will eventually spend all of your time helping them achieve their goals and no time helping yourself to achieve your goals. People that are serious about success will be willing to pay you.

For more information about "Time Management" contact us today at **www.MakeYourLifeEpic.com or call us at 918-851-6920 and we will gladly send you out a daily goal setting work sheet that you can use to help you manage your time more effectively.

*****

Chapter 1:
Marketing

Getting In Front of Likely Buyers In a
Positively, Memorable Way

"In a crowded marketplace, fitting in is failing. In a busy marketplace, not standing out is the same as being invisible."
- Seth Godin (Author of *Purple Cow*)

P lain and simple, marketing is about nothing more than getting your product or service in front of likely buyers in a positively memorable way. Although there has been thousands of books written about marketing that really is all that it's about. When starting a business or growing your existing business, you must come to grips with the fact that marketing is *Super Important.* In fact without effective marketing and a steady stream of customers, nothing else about your business really matters. The fancy LLC. you just setup doesn't matter. The super-detailed "Operating Agreement" doesn't matter. The S-Corp you formed doesn't matter and the new office space you just built out doesn't matter either. Poor marketing makes people poor. Great marketing makes people rich. Mentally marinate on this for a second. Manoj Bhargava's idea to make a five-hour energy shot that tasted like cough syrup wouldn't be worth anything without good marketing. However, because of good marketing this guy went from nothing to something within six months. As of today (2012), this Man's "5-Hour Energy" product is now netting over $300,000,000 per year. Is his product that awesome or is his marketing awesome?

Have you ever found yourself asking questions like, "Why is Meatloaf famous?" "Why were the Kardashians making millions?" "Why is that Ronco guy making millions of dollars per year selling food dehydrators?" My friend it all comes down to marketing. You must remember that it is truly not even possible to give away a great idea or product without good marketing. As an example: Years ago I worked with a company that was absolutely determined to begin selling gourmet dessert items to walk-in clients. They wanted to give away samples of their dessert items in a downtown setting to potential future clients. Thousands of giveaway items were produced and people were paid to pass them out to large crowds of people exiting a major sporting event. Despite the great flavor, the large amount of money and time was invested in their creation, and the overall effort of the team, these items were rejected by masses of people. Of the four people paid to *Give These Gourmet Dessert Items Away*, only one of them actually was able to successfully give them all away. Why? Poor Marketing. The logos weren't obvious and the packaging wasn't consistent. Therefore people didn't trust that these *Free* items were safe. To fans attending this big sporting event it just appeared that four men were passing out homemade baked goods. Were they safe? Were they poisonous? People refused to try them, because the marketing was bad.

Poor marketing will deter would-be customers from buying your products and services because the doubt it inspires. However, excellent marketing has the power to overcome nearly everything, even a poor product. My friend, marketing is nothing more than getting your business, product, or service in front of your target audience in a memorable and meaningful way. That is all marketing is. What are your marketing materials saying about your overall level of excellence? If you have excellent marketing materials, are they making it to your target audience? So who is your target audience? Who is not your target audience? As an example, in the wedding industry, our clients are potential brides-to-be and their mothers. Grooms-to-be almost never call us to inquire about our services. Frankly, most of the grooms are not even aware of nearly any details pertaining to their wedding. They know their wedding date, and they know they get to have sex at the end of this day. They are excited and confident of only these details. This simple truth took me nearly five years to grasp because I did not know what the real definition of marketing was.

Because I didn't know who my target audience was I spent money advertising on radio stations designed for men. As my wife and I worked sixty-five hours per week to make ends meet, I used my precious marketing dollars to buy booths in tradeshows attended by men. I built a website designed for men. I named my wedding packages after things that dudes like. I basically spent my marketing dollars on attempting to reach people like me, because I thought that made sense. Don't be an idiot like I was; take the time to write down the answers to the questions below. Be honest with yourself. If your website is "janky" and does not inspire the level of confidence you want in your "target audience," you must "tame that beast" (fix that website). If you are rocking a mullet as you read this right now, you are going to have to "chop that mop" or your business is going to flop. I used to dress like a member of the "Wu-Tang Clan" (the rap group) when I met with brides and they would never book. I had to change my style in order to get paid. My friend, you might have to "sell out" if you want to ever *Sell Anything* to your "target audience." Answer these questions candidly and honestly and your business will *Boom Baby!*

1) What gender is your target audience?

_____

2) How old is your target audience?

_____

3) What zip codes does your target audience call home?

_____

4) What neighborhoods does your target audience live in?

_____

5) Where does your target audience shop?

_____

6) How old is your target audience?

_____

7) What search terms does your target audience use to "Google Search" for your products and services?

_____

8) What problem(s) does your product / service solve for your target audience?

_____

9) How educated is your target audience?

_____

10) On a scale of 1 to 10 (with 10 being the highest) rank your website's ability to inspire confidence in your target audience: _____

Why?

_____

10) On a scale of 1 to 10 (with 10 being the highest) rank your website's search engine optimization level (does your site come up top in "Google Searches"?): _____

11) On a scale of 1 to 10 (with 10 being the highest) rank your logo and brand's ability to inspire confidence in your target audience: _____

Why?

_____

12) Which of your competition is the most effective at reaching your target audience?

_____

13) Who is the market leader in your industry?

_____

14) What problems do your competition's service / product solve for your target audience?

_____

_____

15) How can your company solve problems for your target audience more effectively than your competition?

_____

_____

16) Who in your industry has a better looking website than your company?

_____

17) Who in your industry has a better looking logo than your company?

_____

18) Who in your industry has better looking overall marketing material than you?

_____

My friend, unless you are not being honest, or unless you are Howard Schultz (the C.E.O. of Starbucks), it looks like you have some work to do. You must beat your competition starting now. Capitalism is a winner-takes-all sport. You are going to either dominate or you are going to be dominated. No pressure here, but if you do not get serious about beating your competition, you are going to raise skinny kids on a skinny budget. Remember as Thomas Edison once said, "Knowledge without application is meaningless." When it comes to marketing you must take the advice from the billionaire and founder of Oracle software company Larry Ellison, "You have to act, and act now."

If you need help with your branding, your social media marketing, your website image, your internet optimization, your print materials and anything related to your overall marketing efforts, we can refer you to America's top service providers. For more information visit **www.MakeYourLifeEpic.com or give us a call today at 918-851-6920 and we will help you do this. For more ideas on how to market effectively to your target audience there are really only three books whose content you need to read and apply, *Guerilla Marketing* by Jay Conrad Levinson, *Think & Grow Rich* by Napoleon Hill and *Soft Selling in A Hard World* by Jerry Vass.

*****

Bonus Profound Truth:
Search Engine Optimization

You must get to the top of Google search results or you won't like your bottom line.

"Everything else becomes unnecessary in a business if nobody sells anything." - Clay Clark (U.S. Small Business Entrepreneur of the Year and America's Most Humble Man)

Bottom line, humans on the planet Earth use "Google" to solve their problems, if they are looking for a product or service, they simply "Google" it. Nearly every research study that is available shows that once people begin their search, they usually only click the first one to five websites that come up in their "organic search" (the non-paid ads). Thus, if your website is not coming up in the first five searches you are going to be losing "that business" to the competition. What makes it worse however, is the fact that nearly every human in America has a smart phone or is getting a smart phone soon. And now people are using their smart phones to "Google Search." Thus, by the time this book is published there will only be about six old ladies and two old dudes (ladies outlive dudes) using phonebooks out there.

Sure, not everybody uses Google, but most people do. Studies show in the United States, well over 85% of all internet searches occur via Google. If you are not a fan of Google, I frankly do not care. I'm not talking about preferences here, I am talking about making money and most people use Google, so focus on it.

My friend, to pour even more gas on this fire, countless studies have also shown that the overwhelming majority of people trust those ridiculous and anonymous reviews posted by people next to your business when it comes up in those "Google Searches". Think about it. Some dude who goes by the internet name (handle) of SALTYDAWG7 can determine whether an actual potential customer pays you or not. Who takes the time to write these comments anyway? Generally the only people with enough time on their hands to write this crap are twenty-seven year-old-man-bear-pigs who live in their mother's basement and spend their afternoons and nights playing Nintendo Wii, World of Warcraft, and Halo. Is this fair? Is this just? Is this the way it should be? No, No, and No. But, this is the way it is. Thus, you can only do three things about it.

1) You can hire someone to get you to the top of the search engine results. I'm not talking about paying for "AdWords". I'm talking about actually getting you to the top of the "Organic Google Search". You can also pay this person to take a proactive approach to your company's online reviews and overall reputation management.

2) You can get yourself to the top of the "Google Search". You can personally take a proactive approach to your company's reputation management.

3) You can do nothing and lose over and over again. You can have skinny kids, using a skinny wallet, and you can complain about how "business is slow" at Chamber of Commerce luncheons.

Folks, this is some serious stuff here. Either you are going to win or you are going to lose here. To quote the former C.E.O. of General Electric, "Ordain your destiny or someone else will."

I am going to assume that you are not a lifeless and ambition free sluggard reading this book just to pass time so I am now going to help you with all three options.

Option #1 - Paying someone to get you to the top of "Google Search" results. This only makes sense if you have more money than time. If you don't, do not pay someone to do this for you. However, if you are going to pay someone do not use the first company you come across. Do not hire a firm to buy "AdWords" on your behalf. "AdWords" *Do Not Determine Your Rank in Google.* Do not hire some company from *India* to do this for you. Call our office today and we will connect you to the Search Engine Optimization companies that we actually use.

Option #2 - Getting yourself to the top of "Google Search" results. This option only makes sense if you have more time than cash. If you are willing to put in the work, this can be one of the best uses of your time out there as a business owner. Once you climb to the top of the "Google Search Results" money will flow into your business if you have the right website design, call script, and overall inquiry conversion system. Your goal is to become the Wikipedia of your local search results for the products and services you offer. Seriously, type the word "dog" into Google right now. Behold, Wikipedia comes up top or near the top does it not? Have you ever asked yourself why this is? Well my friend, you are going to start using Wikipedia as your new template for Search Engine Result goodness. To get to the top of Google results, you must focus on these nine core areas and only these nine core areas.

**Note: If you have no idea what I am talking about, e-mail us at the office today and we will can guide you through this step-by-step process over the phone or in person. However, this chapter will at least orientate you as to what everything on a website is, and how it affects Google search results.

1) Title Tags - You must have localized title tags for your website such as (Tulsa Dog Grooming - Dog Grooming in Tulsa). If you Title Tags are not localized, you cannot win.

2) Keywords - Your website must be filled with the keywords that your potential and current clients are searching for. If your website is about Dog Grooming, then you had better have a lot of keywords related to dog grooming in your website. Type the name of your city plus dog grooming into Google. See what comes up top. Right click on their website and scroll down to "view source." See what your competition is doing. What key words are those guys using? What keywords is Wikipedia using? Get to work my friend!

3) Description - Your website must have the proper description to dominate local search. Right click on your competition's website and scroll down to "view source." See what description those guys are using. You must have a localized description to win.

4) HTML Formatted Websites - If you have a strictly Flash-based website, you will lose. Get an HTML formatted website or enjoy your time at the bottom of search engine results.

5) Inbound Links - Google likes it when reputable sites link to your website. You must get other websites to link to you and there are only four ways to get sites to link to you.

A. You can do some grass-roots networking. Tell people, "Hey man, I will link to your website if you will link to mine." This is a viable option, but it takes time.

B. You can write articles and submit them to various websites that will link back to your website in exchange for the content you provide them.

C. You can use third-party inbound linking sites like "LinkMarket.com" and "SEOLinkVine."

D. You can become the content leader in your industry to the point where people in your industry, media outlets, and others link to you simply because your content is so good (such as Forbes.com).

I recommend that you would focus on options A or B. I also recommend that you hire a college intern to do this work for you. I urge you to tightly manage the Search Engine Optimization (SEO) of your website in a measurable way using the checklists we use. We can e-mail those over to you today if you simply contact us today via **www.MakeYourLifeEpic.com. Request the "SEO Documents" and we will send them right over to you.

6) Outbound links - Google likes it when your website shows that it links to reputable sites. If you are out there linking to a bunch of bogus sites that exists purely to help boost your search engine optimization, this will mess up your search results.

7) Site Mapping - Your website must have a site map at the bottom of it. If your website does not have a site map, Google does not like it. You must make sure that your clients can get to any page of your website from any page on your website quickly. Ask yourself, "Self, what would Wikipedia do?" Look at Wikipedia see how they do it. Look at their links and the huge amount of text content they have. This is why they are number one in a huge number of internet searches.

8) Content - You must have more relevant and original content than your competition. He or she who has the most content will be king of search engine optimization. Make it part of your company's core competency to write thirty minutes worth of original internet content every day. Your competition won't have the diligence to do this and overtime, you will beat them.

9) Inbound Video Link backs - When you post a video to YouTube, you can post a link back to any website in the description. Google likes this. Whenever you post a video, make sure you include a link back to your website. A great site to help spread your videos more effectively is OneLoad.com. Check this site out and begin using it now.

Getting to the top of Google is doable. I have done it with companies time and time again, but the work that goes into the optimization of a website is tedious. However, the results of top Google search results have the power to change your life. We literally helped two different women to more than double the size of their businesses within one year, by helping them get to the top of Google. It is not fun and it takes time and it takes maintenance. Once you build your "search engine optimization house," you still have the mow the lawn every week. You or someone on your staff must focus on creating fresh content daily. Make sure your company writes fresh content on the days that you bathe and groom yourself.

*****

Extra-Special Bonus Profound Truth: Website Conversion

Turn clicks into cash.

"Half the battle is selling music, not singing it. It's the image, not what you sing." - Rod Stewart (Famous Music Chart-Topper and Pop Artist)

If you are going to make *Big Money*, you are going to have to convert the clicks onto your website into cash. Building your website is only half the battle, selling your product is the hard part. We just taught you how to come up in the top of "Google Search Results" but this would be a complete waste of time if your website was not good at converting clicks into cash and online visitors into leads. Getting people to your website is only half the battle. Monetizing each visitor in a way that helps them and helps you is critical. If you don't do this, you will be the large retail store in the mall with the huge lease, which never has anyone available at the cash registers. Eventually, clients begin to get frustrated as they stand in line and before long they just quit coming back.

Although it is as awkward as standing next to the guy who smells bad in a crowded elevator or watching my parents make out on the couch, each year I make my annual trek to Victoria's Secret. I go there to buy my wife lip balm, underwear, and the various other things needed to keep my wife feeling sexy on an annual basis. Whenever I go there, I always take my young kids and I always go during the holidays. And every time I go there is always someone on staff, right there ready to assist me in my speed-shopping adventure of awkwardness. They always have a salesperson that is eager and ready to help me get what I want before my brain explodes due to awkwardness. Your website needs to be as helpful as these sales people. Your

13

website needs to be obvious and it needs to show people in an obvious way where they need to go to get the items and services they want quickly.

Don't make your clients guess at what you do. Don't make a website that screams, "I don't have a purpose and we aren't really sure what we do!" Listed below are my seven rules for website project that you must use on every website creation project you ever undertake.

1. Your Website Must Build Trust and Credibility within Two Seconds

If your website looks "janky" and "amateur," I am simply going to shut down mentally the first time I visit your site. I once did a huge search engine optimization project with one of my clients, only to discover that her actual website looked *Awful* at best. I almost had to staple my forehead when I first saw her site. I was excited to see her top in the local "Google Search" for her category. However, once I clicked on the site, I discovered the "Big Nasty" that was her website. My friend, be real with yourself. If your site does not look *Big Time* you are going to always be *Small Time*. If you have been featured on something, or if you have a photo with some national celebrity, put it on your website. The best example I can think of for making your new site look *Incredible* and *Big Time* from day one is Timothy Ferriss' **www.FourHourWorkWeek.com**. Before he was big his site looked big. And once he got big, his site just continued to look the part.

2. It Must Be Obvious What Problems Your Company / Website Solves Within the First Ten Seconds of Visiting Your Website

If you sell insurance, make it obvious. If you sell real estate, make it obvious. Make it obvious what problems your company solves to the website visitor within the first ten seconds of visiting your website. If your site comes up top in Google, but no one understands what you do or what problems you solve, that is simply not going to work. Customers are less curious than you think.

3. Your Website Must Supply Proof (Facts) That You Can Solve the Visitor's Problems.

Ultimately all sales involves finding the problem, solving the problem, showing that you can and have solved the problems and then prompting the client to action. It is critical that your website demonstrates that you can and have solved problems before. Testimonials are game changing. Testimonials are merely benefits wrapped up in someone else's words. They are powerful. I worked with a client recently who had a client that said something to the effect of, "Since I started working out with Company X, I have lost thirty-two pounds in the past four months. I can fit in my favorite clothes again! Thank you. Thank you. Thank you!" Folks these kinds of comments change the game. Potential customers want to know they are in good hands. Nobody wants to be your experimental project. Nobody wants to be the first client you have tested your theories on. You must demonstrate you have solved these problems before.

4. Contact Information Must Be Obvious

Don't make your clients hunt around your website for ten minutes just to find your phone number and a way to contact you. Don't think that you are being cute by hiding your number. Very few people have the patience to leave voice-mails, to check voice-mails to wait in a fast-food line for more than two minutes, and even less people have the patience to hunt down your phone number that is hidden. Make sure your phone number appears clearly on every page of your website.

5. Your Website Must Offer Great Value and Free Things in Exchange For Contact Information

Naturally, you and I don't want to just give our e-mail address to any random dude because we all know what it is like to wake up each morning to another inbox filled with unwanted E-Mail Spam. However, most people are willing to give their name, phone number and e-mail address in exchange for a *Free E-Book Copy* of *Seven Secrets To Significant Weight Loss* by the 'Personal Trainer of the Stars' John Smith. Most people are willing to submit their name, phone number, and e-mail address in exchange for 25% OFF OF YOUR NEXT PURCHASE simply by registering on our website for our monthly online e-mail catalog. Many people are willing to submit their name, phone number, and e-mail address for a FREE 100 POINT BUSINESS ANALYSIS by the U.S. Small Business Administration Entrepreneur of the Year. Whatever your product or service is you must have *Compelling "Opt-In"* opportunities on every page of your website. You want your website to solve your client's problems and your problems. They want a solution to their problem, but you can't help them if you don't get their contact information.

6. Automated Sales & Follow-up Systems

After someone submits their contact information your system must automatically jump into *Alert Mode*. 24 hours per day your website should send your client and Auto-Responder e-mail "congratulating them on their purchase" or "thanking them for visiting," etc.... Your automated system should begin sending those who chose to "*Opt-In*" weekly newsletters from your business. Your system must be a machine that works while your sleep. Your website must also alert you every time a new deal comes in so that you can call them within five minutes, not five hours. People equate professionalism and quality with speed. Your automated system should make you look really good, really quick.

7. A Shopping Cart That Works

There is a certain percentage of the population that just "prefers to shop online." I found after working with hundreds of businesses, that certain people just like the anonymous, time-efficient method of buying things online. They don't want to develop any relationships over the phone. They don't want to get to know you and they simply want to get what they want and get out. These folks are like the "Self-Checkout Folks" at Wal-Mart that would just prefer to check-out on their own. Don't miss out on these people. Help them help you. Make it easy for them to buy now!

Building a website that looks functionally great that also is compatible with Search Engine Optimization requirements can be challenging and very few web developers are up to the challenge. Most web developers build a site that looks great, but that is never viewed by clients because it was built upon a foundation of internet coding that Google does not recognize. Most web developers don't return phone calls promptly and they specialize in dropping the ball. Thus, to save you the headache, e-mail us today by visiting our website today at **www.MakeYourLifeEpic.com or call us at the office today and we will let you know of the Web Developers that we personally use and who we would recommend.

*****

Super Bonus Profound Truth:
Social Media

Facebook, Twitter, and YouTube who cares and who has the time?...*Your Customers!*

"It's never the platform, it's always the message." - Gary Vaynerchuk (Author of *Crush It!*, Social Media Guru and Serial Entrepreneur)

My friends, the internet has given more and more power to the people. Some people in San Francisco did not agree with the way that their subway system was being managed, so they hacked into the system and published the personal information of members of the law enforcement community. Social Media is massive and it is growing. Recent studies are now showing time and time again that people are staying connected to their Facebook all day. When they are awake, they are connected via their smart phones. Now more than ever, your company has to "stay in conversation" with your clients. They will post comments on your *Facebook's* "Wall". They will *Tweet* you a complaint. They will post comments on your *YouTube* videos. Clients want to stay in this "conversation" with companies they like.

Today, people want a company to showcase their personalities. If you only talk *at* your clients and potential clients, you will irritate your clients and they will move on a company that is more willing to converse with them. Does this sound fun? I personally don't think so. It drives me nuts personally. But, it is not up to me and because this is the case. We are going to have to converse with our clients starting now. However, to keep your brain from exploding you must focus only on the big three. Sure there are tons of Social Media sites out there, but you are going to be Tweeting about your homelessness if all you do is post on your Social Media every day. Find the balance my friend.

**If social media is over-whelming to you and you have no idea what I am talking about because you are too busy making money to mess with this stuff give our team a call today and they will recommend America's top Social Media service providers for you. Don't get stuck with an unreliable service provider.

1) YouTube - Your company really needs to post YouTube content on a weekly basis at a minimum. This footage does not have to be great, but it does have to fit in with your company's brand and identity. One great way to leverage your time here is to record fifty-two (one-minute) videos all at one time. Change your shirt, change your topic, but record it all on one day. This will help you leverage your time better. Just upload the videos once per week and you are good. Make sure to title your videos something that people actually search for and you are good to go.

Your company must have a dedicated YouTube Channel. Your company must have a fully-filled out YouTube profile and your company must post videos every week.

2) Facebook - Your company needs a business page. You simply have to have one. If you don't you run the risk of looking like the ninety-year-old guy at a sorority pool party. It is just weird. For examples of what your company's Facebook page should look like, simply do a "Google Search" for Terrell Owens. Terrell is a former N.F.L. star player and he makes his living and stays relevant by Tweeting, and constantly posting on Facebook.

Your company must post to its "Facebook Wall" at least once per week. It must respond to comments diligently. You must have a fully filled-out profile.

3) Twitter - Your company needs a fully-filled out Twitter profile page and you must post at least once per week. Great brands post every day. Posting every day is great, but only if your team is willing to converse with people that want to interact with your company.

All other social media platforms will just make your brain explode. Make sure you implement Social Media marketing as a part of your company's overall marketing strategy. You must stay in touch with your clients while building your brand and your company's loyalists.

**If you need help with your social media management you can also contact our team through our website at www.MakeYourLifeEpic.com. The best book ever written about social media marketing is *Crush It* by Gary Vaynerchuk.

*****

Chapter 2:
Sales

Sales - Without them, nothing else matters

"A great idea sells itself" - Someone Stupid

Whether it is fair or not, every successful entrepreneur really has two professions. They are a salesman and an accountant. They are a salesman and an engineer. They are a salesman and the President. They are a salesman and a bakery owner. They are a salesman and a realtor. They are a salesman and an insurance agent, or they are an employee only. If you are serious about succeeding as an entrepreneur you must become passionate about learning to persuade others.

The best leaders in business, religion, politics, and music are usually the best sales people around. Our Presidential debates are hilarious. More than half of Americans no longer have any idea of where they stand on any core issues and we sit there on our couches watching and judging each candidate to see who is the best at persuading. We want to see which candidate is the best salesman, and then we call them, "the most Presidential."

Why don't we just look at their records and vote based on that? Their records are statements of fact right?

Either they voted for this or they didn't. Either they did this or not. However, as humans we aren't interested in facts alone, we are interested in one's ability to influence others. On occasion we are so fascinated with one's ability to "sell" and "persuade" others that we will actually ignore all logic, all truth, and all factual information simply to fill the emotional need being created by a skilled persuader, gifted speaker or talented salesperson.

Think of some of the purchases we make. If you bought a $150,000 house did you really make money? Did you really come out ahead? Unless you bought that home from somebody who had to sell their home at some deep discount because they were financially hurting you will probably lose money on this home purchase. I'm sure the talented realtor probably used their hypnotic blend of Jedi sales tricks, smiles, humor and half-truths to compel you take action. To appeal to you emotionally, your realtor probably told you things like:

**For the record, I am not just against real estate in general. I have been part-owner of a real estate company.

"Your interest on your loan is 100% tax deductible"

"A home is truly the biggest investment you can ever make in your future."

"The value of your home rises every year."

"There has never been a better time to buy."

"You're going to be living the American dream."

"It's a good deal."

But upon closer examination let's just see if you actually made money on this "good deal" that was the "best investment you could ever buy."

- Purchase Price = $150,000.00

- Commission to Realtor (Realtors) = $9,000.00

- Closing Costs = $4,500.00

- Down Payment = $15,000.00

- Number Years You Pay Nearly 100% Interest Only Payments Before You Actually Begin Paying Towards the Principle on a 30 Year Loan = 15

- Years the Average America Lives In A Home = Less Than 5

- Commission To Realtor (Realtors) When You Sell the House 5 Years Later = $9,000.00

- Did you actually make money? No. Home much did you lose? I will let you do the math...But unless you bought this house without a realtor and unless you bought this house as a foreclosure, and unless you used a fifteen-year loan and unless you lived in the house for a long time you did not make money. But at least you felt "emotionally good" before I told you this stuff.

My friend, nearly all major purchases and decisions are made by people for emotional reasons and your goal as an honest salesperson is to prove how your product or service can help your clients feel the way they want to feel, because your product or service will deliver the results for them that they need to solve their problems now.

The idea that great ideas will simply sell themselves is bogus. Even if you had a real and unbelievable product, you would not be able to impact the world if you could not "persuade" Americans of its attributes, of its "believability" and its problem solving abilities. I recently spoke at a University that had assembled an all-star lineup of speakers who were millionaires and who all had great information that every college student on the campus needed to hear. If millionaire alumni are teaching you specifically how they became millionaires and what you can do to become a millionaire as well, shouldn't all college students attend this event? However and sadly enough, less than fifty students attended the event because it was so poorly "sold" to the students of the campus as being the "place to be." I recently worked with another University who struggles to grow enrollment year after year simply because their marketing team consists of bureaucrats, paper pushers, and people who couldn't influence a starving person to take a free meal if they had to.

America had to be attacked by the Japanese before our country could be "persuaded" that the Jewish people were really being slaughtered in mass. However, Hitler was able to use his masterfully evil "skills of persuasion" to motivate an entire country to nearly exterminate and entire race of people. This sick bastard nearly convinced an entire people group that hyper-inflation and the devaluation of their money supply and the destruction of their economy was the entire fault of the Jewish people. He needed the help of propaganda expert and film maker Joseph Gobles, but he pulled off the great evil known as the "Holocaust" bases solely on his power to "influence" others.

25

Ray Croc had to work tirelessly to convince business owners that buying a duplicatable and scalable restaurant was a good idea. Walt Disney lost everything he had once and almost lost it all again trying to convince the world that his "Magical Kingdom" was not just some delusional dream. Steve Jobs was fired from Apple (the company he started), because he struggled to convince the world that they needed his company's products and services. My friend, if you cannot show the world what problems your product solves, you are going to fail. If you cannot show people time and time again how your product makes their life easier, better, simpler, more fun, more exciting, safer, etc.... You will fail. You must be able to sell or your business will fail.

Thus, I ask you this question passionately. What are fifty ways that your company's product or service solves problems? If you can't come up with fifty, I encourage you to quit or to find someone else to sell your product for you. Bill Gates hired Paul Allen to do this selling for him. Maybe you too need to hire someone? However, if selling is not one of your companies' core competencies, you are doomed, unless you are willing to learn this skill.

This is not a gifting, this is skill. "Persuasion" (sales) is something that I have taught to thousands of people. And it's not like I'm only training America's intellectual elite here. A few years back I taught one gentlemen to sell who was working as an inbound call representative at a local call center. He was making $7.00 per hour to answer the questions people had about why their satellite TV was not working. He graduated from high school and hadn't read a book since. Yet, he listened, took notes and applied the principles and 3 months later he was making nearly $1,500 per week. We taught these principles to a Starbuck's Barista who had converted his body in a human tattoo exhibit and within just a matter of months he transformed his local store into one of the top bagged coffee retailers in the country. I have taught insurance salesman, appliance store owners, accountants, aspiring ministers, web developers, and people from all walks of life how to use the "power of persuasion." I personally struggled mightily just to pass the ACT tests to get into college and even I learned these skills. My friend YOU CAN LEARN THIS! Just like *Jedi* powers, this "power of persuasion" can be used for good or evil. Sincerely, you must be careful how you use these moves, when you use these moves and who you share these moves with. Let's not create another Hitler.

To "persuade" anyone, to do anything, you must begin with the end in mind. Before you interact with your client you must clearly know your objective. Your object should be to get them to take action and to make a commitment to either meet again at an agreed upon time or to buy something.

The system that I have developed for this is the best sales system available today. This book is designed to get right to the point, but if you need more information I highly recommend you purchase, *Soft Selling in a Hard World* by Jerry Vass. His systematic approach to selling is profound. To save you over a decade of research, studying and experimenting might system is a synthesis of the "best practice" sales techniques that are out there today. The entire program has put together using material from America's top sales professionals and organizations including: Dell Computers, IBM, Farmers Insurance, Shane Harwell, Jeffrey Gittomer, Brian Tracy, Chet Holmes, Shane Harwell, Paul Arnold, Dale Carnegie and many, many more.

Without any further ado, here is the system:

Step 1: Establish Rapport

The Goal of Establishing Rapport: Get the client to like & trust you.

Rule #1: Let the client talk 70% of the time.

Rule #2: Control the conversation and get them talking by asking skilled questions.

Rule #3: Demonstrate your mastery by asking thought-provoking questions that expose the buyer's lack of knowledge on your subject.

Rule #4: Establish yourself as the expert through the way you dress, look, and carry yourself.

Rule #5: Never spend more than five minutes building rapport.

Rule #6: Use humor throughout.

Rule #7: Script out your entire presentation and use it every time.

Step 2: Discover Needs

The Goal of Discovering Needs: The goal is to create a dissatisfaction gap by helping your client to discover where they are currently at and where they ideally want to be. You must help the client to discover that they have a problem if you are going to be able to sell them your solutions (products or services).

Rule #1: Ask the client questions to discover what their one year and five year goals are.

Rule #2: Ask the client questions that expose areas of weakness in your competition.

Rule #3: Ask the client questions that showcase your knowledge of your product / service and your client's lack of understanding of your product / service.

Rule #4: Ask questions that inspire confidence in your business by contrast to the competition.

Rule #5: Assume nothing; ask questions so that you truly know who are dealing with.

Rule #6: Never spend more than seven minutes determining your client's needs.

Rule #7: Use humor throughout.

Rule #8: Script out your entire presentation and use it every time.

Step 3: Solve the Client's Problem (Benefits)

The Goal of Solving the Client's Problem: Effectively demonstrate how your company can uniquely solve the client's problem.

Rule #1: Know, memorize, and become passionate about four benefits that differentiate your company from the competition.

Rule #2: Follow every benefit and every problem you solve for the client with a statement of fact.

Rule #3: Never say something that you cannot prove. In your print material, on the phone and anywhere you market your products or services, you must provide verifiable proof that your company can and will deliver the solutions you are selling.

Rule #4: Every benefit you give should explain to client both the "gain aspects of using your company" and the "pain aspects of not using your company."

Rule #5: Nuance the delivery of each benefit you give to client in a way that meets the unique needs we learned they have during the discovery portion of your presentation.

Rule #6: Always present your benefits (backed by provable facts) in writing via a sales book or brochure. People find everything to be more believable when it is in print.

Rule #7: Never spend more than three minutes presenting how your company can solve the client's problems (benefits).

Rule #8: Use humor throughout.

Rule #9: Script out your entire benefits (problem solving) portion of your presentation and use it every time.

Rule #10: Your potential clients and nearly all humans don't want to hear about the features of your products and services. They want to hear about how you can solve their problems. Don't confuse features with benefits. Don't fill up your brochure with technical jargon that only industry insiders know. Don't fill up your brochures and marketing materials with non-compelling text and claims that are unsupported. Saying that "we are the most professional" is much like me claiming that "I'm the nicest guy in my neighborhood" while talking to a bunch of church friends.

The statement "we are the most professional" carries absolutely zero weight.

Step 4: Call to Action

The Goal of Prompting Your Client to Take Action: You must get the prospective client to commit to taking action via appointment within 72 hours of your last interaction with them.

Rule #1: You must overcome the procrastination objection every time. Whether you are attempting to sell something, trying to get a bunch of couples over for dinner or working on getting your entire family to take a vacation cruise for the holidays you must aggressively focus on overcoming the procrastination objection. Put simply most people never take action to do anything unless they are prompted. You must prompt your people to take action or you will never get paid.

Rule #1: Assume that every client wants to "take the next step."

Rule #2: Never ask the client directly if they want to buy from you.

Rule #3: Never ask the client a yes or no question; always give them an A or B option.

Rule #4: Your goal as a salesman is to get a commitment to either meet again or to "take the next step" during every appointment.

Rule #5: Always sound confident when going for the call to action, never begin talking softly and awkwardly before you ask for a commitment.

Rule #6: Every appointment is a waste of time and is completely meaningless if it does not result in a commitment to "take the next step."

Rule #7: Always work via appointment only, because "my day timer is so slammed right now" get in the habit of saying, "because my day timer is so slammed right now and I know that you stay busy, when is the best time to connect with you? At _____ or _____?"

Rule #8: Every call to action should occur within seventy-two hours of your last interaction with the client. NEVER ALLOW MORE THAN 72 HOURS TO PASS when you are pursuing the close of a deal.

Rule #9: Never spend more than one minute calling the client to take action.

Rule #10: Use humor throughout.

Rule #11: Script out your entire call to action portion of your sales presentation and use it every time.

Are you thinking this system might just not work for you? Well, here is a little faith booster for you. Over the years I have trained countless companies on how to implement the sales system described above. And every time that this sales system has actually been implemented with pig-headed determination by the leadership team they have witnessed amazing results. In fact we have trained an implemented this system for major college fund-raising, ministry fund-raising, appliance sales, retail sales, apparel sales, photography sales, bakery sales, video production sales, lending, commercial real estate, supplement sales, and nearly any sector of the market place can you can think of. This system produces near "magic" results.

My friend, the system cannot work unless you do. Remember, you get paid based on the results you produce, not the results you intend on producing. Napoleon Hill once said, "Action is the real measure of intelligence." So the question is ultimately about how intelligent you are.

To get a copy of a quality sales script, to get help writing an effective sales script, or for more information about effective sales scripting systems contact our team through **www.MakeYourLifeEpic.com or purchase *Soft Selling in a Hard World* by Jerry Vass. This book explains to you the step-by-step process of creating a sales system that works.

*****

Spectacular Bonus Profound Truth:
Sales Tracking

If it is not measurable it is not manageable.

"Face reality as it is, not as it was or as you wish it to be." - Jack Welch

It is absolutely critical that you and your team know where each and every inquiry source comes from! It is important for you to know how many calls your sales team is making per day! It is important for you to know with 100% certainty how many meaningful conversations your sales team is having each day. It is important for you to know how many appointments your sales team is setting up each day. It is *Super Important* for you to know what your team's appointment to closed deals ratio is. It is unbelievably important for you to know what each sales person's average "ticket price" or "sales price" is. Which one of your sales people is the best? Which salesperson needs the most training? What marketing pieces work and what marketing pieces do not? Which mailers are effective and which are not? Is your Google AdWords program generating you money or costing you money? You must track all of the details related to each and every sale, and prospective sale for your organization if you are going to effectively manage it. DON'T BE AN IDIOT. TRACK THIS INFORMATION!

If you want to guarantee continual mediocrity, then don't worry about tracking. If you want to improve your team you must be able to face the reality as it truly is. You must be able to confront the good and bad realities you face so that you can make the necessary plans to take your company to the next level. Trust me on this. Before I got wise and began to study and implement the genius of sales gurus like Jerry Vass, Chet Holmes, Shane Harwell, and others I was continually managing by guess work. I would spend an entire afternoon working with a sales guy on prospecting when he in fact had no problem prospecting. He needed a ton of work on how to convert and appointment into a "booked deal", but I never talked or trained about that because I didn't know my numbers. Today, I now know the numbers to the point where I can pull a sales person aside and coach them to victory because I know specifically where they are struggling.

We cannot blame good people for not producing results in a system in which it is not possible to succeed because the training methods are wrong. If you don't track your numbers your sales numbers will be volatile, your trainings will not address the root of most problems, and you might get a nose bleed. Take control of your life starting now; don't wait forever to take action like I did.

It's embarrassing to put in writing, but I did not implement the sales tracking systems until my business almost crumbled while I went on seven-day Caribbean Cruise vacation with my incredible wife and our only child at the time (Havana). Before hopping onto the cruise boat I was confident that our team would continue producing *Big Results* on the sales floor during my absence. However, upon returning to the DJ Connection office lair, much to my horror I was confronted with a much more harsh reality. As a team, their numbers were terrible.

During the seven days I was gone, the sales numbers had dropped by at least 50% below our weekly averages. This was unacceptable, and I wanted to rush in to fix the problem, but I didn't know who the problem people were. I didn't know who set bogus appointments, who didn't set appointments, who worked hard, who didn't work hard, whose closing percentage was high or whose closing percentage was low. As I frantically worked to discover the source of the problem, I repeatedly discovered that without tracking our team did not have true accountability. It seemed as though each guy on our team had a different person to blame or a different outside variable to attribute their lack of success to. It was then that I discovered that my lack of tracking was creating a huge lack of accountability. And this lack of accountability was causing a serious lack of productivity. My friend, Jack Welch, arguably one of America's top C.E.O.s of all time, once famously wrote, "Face reality as it is, not as it was or as you wish it to be." If you aren't currently tracking your sales, you must commit to the action steps needed to implement a tracking system right now. When are you going to start?

For more information about how to implement an award-winning sales program, I highly recommend reading, *The Ultimate Sales Machine* by Chet Holmes. If you want to save yourself the read and you just want to get results now, call us up at 918-851-6920 or send us an e-mail via our website at **www.MakeYourLifeEpic.com.

*****

Chapter 3:
Customer Service

Turning your customers into apostles

"Do what you do so well that they will want to see it again and bring their friends." - Walt Disney (The guy who turned his drawings of a mouse into a magical media empire)

M y friend, as you travel around the "Wheel of Wealth" you will find that it works. In fact you will find it working so well that you will begin to feel uncomfortable with the huge amounts momentum being generated. I liken this feeling of uncontrolled growth to the feelings that those crazy race car drivers must have each year as they race around Colorado's great Pike's Peak. You will be filled with adrenaline as you race up the mountain, but you will also be aware that there are no guard rails and that one bad turn will kill you. Don't *Freak Out*, but if you do I get it! In fact most entrepreneurs have had a mental break down or two and that's because you have people in your race car with you. Your family and your employees depend upon your ability to win this race while not dying. However, if you are going to win this race, you must keep your eyes on the road. *Again, It is Worth Repeating. Keep Your Eyes on the Road!* What is this road? The road is customer service!

In every business your customers are the road. Your customers are the life blood of your business. Without your customers you have nowhere to go. In fact, without your life blood, you won't have a life. Without them you are dead. Nearly every organization I have had the privilege of working with focuses on everything, but sales. If these weren't real people it would be hilarious. But because these people have real kids and real families, it is just sad.

To perfectly demonstrate the insanity of this mindset, I have one business coaching horror story that comes to mind. I was once hired by a real estate company to oversee their rebranding and overall marketing strategy. Within two hours of working with them and interviewing their 8 sales people I was shocked to discover that nobody had closed a single deal for an entire year. Here they wanted to spend their time focusing on improving their image in the community and their overall brand, and yet almost no one on staff ever returned calls to inquiring customers or existing customers. The one sales professional I was working with was absolutely obsessed with everything other than making sure that her clients were happy. Her entire focus was on the state of the economy and the gift bags she wanted us to give to the members of the media. These people could spend hours talking about anything, but when I asked them about how what tenants thought about them and how we could improve our overall customer service, they suddenly grew quiet. It became apparent that they had never devoted any time to keeping existing clients happy. If clients pay us they are essentially the boss. So wouldn't it be a good idea to systematically wow them at every opportunity?

The goal of great customer service should be to turn every client into a wowed client. Your goal should be to turn those bearded friends of yours into Apostles. My friend, Jesus had this whole customer service thing down. He washed their feet. He sacrificed his life for theirs. He did more than he asked them to do. You must always keep in mind that wealth creation is nothing more than an on-going value exchange with your client base. The more value you give them, the more they will be willing to pay you. So how will you enhance your customer's experience? How do you add the most value to them? I will now show you how.

Rule #1: Think like Walt Disney.

Mr. Disney believed that you should treat your clients like celebrities and honored guests at your magical kingdom. Write down a list of ideas you have to treat existing clients like honored guests at your magical kingdom:

_____

_____

_____

_____

_____

Rule #2: Make your kingdom smell magically marvelous and not like a porcelain palace.

Your place of business must smell good, not hood. The people who work for you must smell good. Your business has to smell good. The smell of cat pee is not going to work here. If you are working out of your house, you must make sure you and your business smell good. If your business smells like a city park bathroom, you are done. Ladies make the majority of purchases and they will not come back if your bathroom is sicker than "Swine Flu"! What are the action steps you will do to make sure that your business and your team smell magical every day?

_____

_____

_____

_____

_____

Rule #3: Treat every word your clients say as though it were a profound statement.

When your clients talk, listen. When your clients complain, ask them how you can do better, don't justify. When your clients praise you, thank them. When your clients speak, hang on their every word. Love on your clients. Treat them like a fiancé treats his bride-to-be. Woo them. What are the action steps you will do to make sure you and your people are held accountable to treating your clients like lovers?

_____

_____

_____

_____

_____

Rule #4: Over-Deliver to each and every client.

Give the clients more than they paid for every time and you won't have to worry about advertising. Make it one of your company's core marketing strategies to systematically exceed the expectations of every client. If you offered them four hours of service, give them five. Find a way to exceed their expectations. When you exceed their expectations you activate the universal power found with the "Law of Reciprocity". Without getting too deep here, the person you over-delivered for now has a sub-conscious responsibility to "pay you back". They might not even realize that they feel this way, but people who have a soul (Non-Satan worshippers) will find themselves having a strong urge to refer your business once they discover that you did more than you promised. They may feel the urge to mail you a tip. They may feel the need to call in "just to thank you."

Nearly zero companies ever over-deliver systematically, which is why we always remember the ones that do. We always remember Southwest Airlines, QuikTrip, Starbucks, U.P.S., and the Disney. However, we struggle to remember the other companies. We always remember the barista (coffee server at Starbucks) named "Iesha" who took the time give our daughter a free birthday dessert. She didn't have to do that, which is why we love that she did.

How will your company systematically over-deliver to each and every client?

_____

_____

_____

_____

_____

Rule #5: Treat your best clients differently.

Aren't we supposed to treat all clients the same? Only if you want to be poor. If you have a client that refers you and your business over and over again, you had better show this person special attention. If you have a client that uses your services over and over again, you had better celebrate this client. You had better call this client to personally thank them. You had better send a pizza to their place of business or a gift card to them during the holidays. Your top clients needed to be treated with a special attention that is over and above your normally incredibly high customer service standards. On a practical level, you don't have the time or money to send every client a Christmas card, a gift card, and a gift basket. However, you can always find time to go the *Extra Mile* beyond the *Extra Mile* for the clients that are exponentially growing your business. How are you going to go the extra mile, beyond the extra mile for your top clients?

_____

_____

_____

_____

_____

Rule #6: Be an enemy of anyone who treats your customers badly.

If you are a human, you have probably found yourself rushing to someone's defense at one time or another. If someone is harassing your wife, you probably had a strong desire to rearrange their face. If someone made fun of your baby sister, you probably had a strong sense of urgency about introducing their face to a metal pipe. My friend, if any one of your employees disrespects your customers, they are now an enemy of your state. Assume that they have made an innocent mistake and dig into the issue, but if they are consistently making your clients wait, irritating your clients or otherwise ruining your relationships with clients, they must be dealt with swiftly.

Have the fortitude, the tenacity and the courage of your convictions to discipline and fire employees that don't revere the profound importance of your relationships with your clients. However, if you have more than fifty people working for you like I do, it will be impossible for you to individually monitor everyone. Thus you must implement a merit-based pay system based around "mystery shoppers" or "client survey and satisfaction feedback."

You must systematically take time out to ask your clients, "How are we doing?" The QuikTrip convenience store chain has mystery shoppers that go into each store on a regular basis. Bonuses and promotions hinge upon these anonymous reviews. These mystery shoppers could be coming in at any time and employees of QuikTrip never know who they are. Our businesses survey every client and ask them to rate their overall satisfaction with our sales and customer service team. Bonuses and promotions hinge upon this survey feedback. Essentially the message should be, "if you want to get promoted and make more money, start by wowing our clients!"

What are the action steps you will take to hold your team accountable to treating your clients like the incredibly important people they are?

_____

_____

_____

_____

What is the process you will create to deal with employees that upset your clients?

_____

_____

_____

_____

Setting up these systems early on in the creation of your new business is absolutely essential to building a strong business upon which your company can grow and thrive. However you must remember that my team and your team, and anybody's team of employees will never respect what you don't inspect. The famous minister, Bishop Carlton Pearson taught me this little phrase that has served me well, "You must inspect what you expect." At the end of the day you must make a daily checklist *That Is Inspected by Management* for any operations that you want your team to actually implement. It's frustrating I know, but I'm telling you from first-hand experience that leadership and sales expert Dale Carnegie was correct when once famously wrote, "When dealing with people, remember you are not dealing with creatures of logic, but with creatures bristling with prejudice, and motivated by pride and vanity."

All humans are motivated by the desire to avoid pain and the desire to obtain gains, so make sure you incorporate these management aspects into the creation of your customer service systems or they will just become ideals that your team never lives up to. To really hammer home this point, I will give you one example from one of the businesses coaching clients I worked with years ago.

At this particular business they prepared and served gourmet food. In fact, everything about their website, their marketing materials, their music, their branding material, their packages, and the way they dealt with people was designed to justify their high-price point as a gourmet food provider. After we helped this business develop their systems they actually had everything in place they needed to succeed. They were featured on TV countless times, they were top in Google and their phones rang constantly. Their dramatically increased revenue had actually allowed them to even expand to a nice new location where they had more physical space available to increase production capacity. These guys had everything in place to experience huge profits. However, we soon discovered that they were not being diligent about making sure that the company's daily checklists were being filled out and inspected by a manager. Because of this they started to "drop the ball" consistently. Floors weren't being swept, product was not being inspected before it was delivered to the client and things began to fall apart. MY FRIEND, THIS BUSINESS AND ALL YOUR BUSINESS VENTURES WILL FAIL IF YOU DO NOT HAVE THE DILIGENCE NEEDED TO INSPECT WHAT YOU WANT PEOPLE TO RESPECT. IF YOU DON'T SET HIGH-STANDARDS AND FORCE PEOPLE TO MEET YOUR HIGH-STANDARDS YOUR BUSINESS WILL ALWAYS FAIL TO ACHIEVE ANYTHING BEYOND MEDIOCRITY BECAUSE MOST PEOPLE ARE CONTENT WITH BEING MEDIOCRE.

Like all businesses, over time, the owners' vision and ideals digressed into suggestions to be implemented only when convenient. Within a few weeks, these suggestions were regarded by the staff as mere opinions. And soon the opinions became things that the employees simply grew comfortable with not doing at all. Paychecks continued to be written and the employees continued to be paid. Gradually, the gourmet atmosphere had deteriorated into a "garage sale atmosphere." The overhead music that they had invested so much time in creating was no longer being played. The staff uniforms were no longer being worn. And the daily cleaning checklists were not being implemented. This cycle of deterioration continued on and on and on until one of their customers actually discovered an old and dead cricket on the floor of the dining area. This customer was horrified. And this customer never came back. The owner was then forced to confront a series of issues all at once. These great systems that been created had now completely disappeared into the vast abyss known as the "Sea of Intentions." The sales had begun to drop off dramatically. The owner had to ask himself, was it the food? Was it the location? Was it the sales team or was it simply a lack of *Inspecting What He Was Expecting*? Quickly things had to change and the owner had to get back to the basics or his business would fail. All of sudden the importance of creating and inspecting the daily checklists I had been talking about made sense. The owner had to take action immediately.

Driven by the fear of failure and the desire to succeed the owner began being pig-headed about inspecting these daily checklists. The owner made sure to communicate that the managers who have to inspect 100% of the daily checklists if they wanted to receive 100% of their paychecks. Things began to change. The company began to win again. My friend, this story is all too common. Don't let this situation happen to you.

For more information about how to initially setup a merit-based pay system read, the Harvard case studies and conclusions found within the book entitled, *Service Profit Chain* by James L. Heskett, W. Earl Sasser, and Leonard A. Schlesinger. If you have more money than time, visit **www.MakeYourLifeEpic.com or call us today at 918-851-6920 and we fly out to your place of business to efficiently build this system for you.

*****

Chapter 4:
Service / Product Wow

You must systematically exceed the expectations of your clients to grow exponentially.

"Expect more than others think possible." - Howard Schultz - Visionary and Founder of Starbucks

Now assuming that you have already crafted a business that makes money on paper after doing a detailed costing analysis, let's move on to the fun stuff.

Napoleon Hill once wrote, "Over-deliver and you will soon be overpaid". Hill was stating the obvious, yet often forgotten truth that customers will be glad to give you free exponential-growth-causing "word of mouth" if you are willing to exceed their expectations with your product or service. Doing this is not hard, but it does require diligence. In Proverbs 21:5 (NIV), it is written, "The plans of the diligent lead to profit as surely as haste leads to poverty." Sam Walton the famous business mogul and founder of retail giant Wal-Mart once famously said, "There is only one boss. The customer. And he can fire everybody in the company from the chairman on down, simply by spending his money somewhere else." My friends, your service and product must wow your customers. Your product and service must wow humans or it will fail, and because we are operating our businesses on the planet Earth, you will have to wow them in a profitable way. You can't simply just throw huge sums of money and bribery at the customers to earn their business, unless you are a political candidate (sorry, I had to get that in somewhere). Think about the truly amazing customer service experiences out there today. Take Starbucks and Southwest Airlines for instance.

When you walk into a Starbucks you are greeted by a "Barista" not just an employee. Your drink is customized for your unique palette and flavor preferences. Your name is written on the cup to even further enhance the experience. The drinks are referred to as Tall, Venti, and various other unique nomenclatures. The fact they don't have small, medium and large actually ads to the perceived value and experience. What does it cost to change the words your team uses to refer to sizes of things? What would it cost your team to write the name of your clients on their cups? How much value does this add? Southwest Airlines offers unassigned seating to make the seating process go quicker. Flight attendants are encouraged to be funny. In fact, they actually celebrate and reward the most innovative, unique, and spirited flight attendants by featuring them in commercials and featuring them in their own magazine they produce for the passengers viewing pleasure while flying. Southwest gives bonuses to their most spirited employees. They don't charge extra for bags. How much does this cost them? How much will this cost you? Do the math. Take the time. Figure out what is going to wow your clients while producing a nice profit for you and your team. Ultimately the prices that your customers will be willing to pay will be based upon the perceived value that they believe your product or service offers them. The more you write their names on a cup, the more they will be willing to pay. Starbucks gets away with charging a large sum of money for each coffee because they offer a large amount of value. However, I must warn you. If you do not add value to customers in a systematic and memorable way, they will be forced to make their purchasing decisions based on prices alone, and this places you in the commodities market and this is not a good place to be. Always remember that when value is absent pricing concerns and objections will become super prevalent. Take ten minutes and write down all of the benefits that your chief competition offers and how you will systemically "best them" or "one up them" and you will win.

Benefits your competitors offer and how you will "out do them" with your service:

_____

_____

_____

_____

_____

_____

_____

_____

_____

_____

_____

_____

_____

_____

_____

_____

_____
_____
_____
_____

_____
_____
_____
_____

_____
_____
_____
_____

_____
_____
_____
_____

_____
_____
_____
_____

If you have completed the above exercise and you find yourself unable to correctly price your services or products I would highly recommend that you do one of two things. Option one, spy on your competition and then do more than they do for less than they charge. Option two, call up to our office and schedule an in-depth pricing, and value-add brainstorming session with our team. In less than two hours we can help you build a pricing model that makes sense for both you and your customers.

If you need help beating your competition, and you can't find someone who is willing to spy on your competition on your behalf our firm will be happy to "mystery shop" or "spy on them" for you. Visit **www.MakeYourLifeEpic.com or give us a call today at 918-851-6920 and we will help you do this. For more ideas on how to wow your clients, read *Soft Selling in a Hard World* by Jerry Vass.

Bonus Profound Truth:
Duplicatability

If it's not duplicatable and scalable, it's not worth doing.

"Most entrepreneurs are merely technicians with an entrepreneurial seizure. Most entrepreneurs fail because you are working In your business rather than On your business." - Michael Gerber

If you have created a product or service that only you or an elite few can do, you have not created a *Viable Business to Get Rich. You Have Created a Job* that no one will want. Unless you are offering some rare service like being famous doctor who performs rare surgeries on the throwing shoulders of pitchers and NFL quarterbacks it will be very hard for you to achieve riches if your business model if you are the only person who can deliver the product or service. If you are the only person in your company who can render the product or service, you are going to have to work all the time and people will always ask for you personally. If you have a design company and you are the only designer on staff that you can ever trust, this is a problem. If you start a D.J. company and you are the only "good entertainer" this is a problem. You must create a product or service that is easily scalable and duplicatable.

If you can't train someone to do tasks needed to perform their job in forty hours or less, you have a big problem. How would you grow quickly if it takes you two years to train people "to do it your way"? I meet entrepreneurs all the time who have been in business for twenty-five years who don't get this. I met a dude recently who is an older photographer and he actually said, "In my company, I don't just trust anybody to take photos. In fact, that is why I take all of the photos myself for all of my clients." This is *Blasphemy* for any successful entrepreneur. After a workshop I spoke at I was approached by an older gentlemen who said, "Yeah well my business is different. It takes over a year to train someone to fix computers the way we do it." I didn't want to argue with him in front of his peers, but how sad is that worldview? First off, who in their right mind would want to train for one year to learn how to repair computers for a company in which you can only make $28,000 per year if you are good. Unless you are trying someone to become a bi-lingual nuclear submarine operator, you simply cannot take this much time to train someone how to deliver your products or services. What if the person you are training quits half-way through the year? What if they decide to move? What if you have to fire them? If it takes you one year to train someone you'll be 87 years old when you finally get your team built.

If You Are Going to Make Big Money, you are going to have to delegate everything but the crucial decision making. This photographer needs to quit calling himself an entrepreneurship before he demotivates everybody around him.

I realize that the process of building a duplicatable process seems daunting, however you can do this. I took Algebra three times and I never did pass my C.P.R. class. Math, memorization and things that involve the sciences are generally tough for me, so I can tell you with confidence; if I can learn to do this then I know you can learn how to do this. As you begin to create this duplicatable system just keep three quick rules of thumb in mind and you will be off and running.

1) Common sense is not common - Whenever you find yourself saying, "That should be common sense" go ahead and get out the stapler and staple a Post-It Note to your forehead to remind yourself not to do this. If you are truly creating a service or product that does add tremendous value to people's lives then your customers currently should not be experiencing these unique value adds elsewhere in the marketplace already. Thus, your employees most certainly have not seen these high-value systems in action either.

2) You must be able to train someone to do every core competency within forty hours or less - The system that you build should be easy to train and it should be written down. I am always amazed by the businesses I work with that claim to have a "unique system" or the "best staff processes," but upon further examination you realize that everything the company does is not written down, and thus it does not happen systematically. Imagine if the Bible was just a verbal history. That would be one crazy book at this point. You must write things down. You must turn your value-add thoughts into things.

3) You must condense value-add into a series of checklists to be appropriately delegated - If your systems consist of huge lengthy binders and documents, congratulations, you are going to be the only one who will ever read these! You must turn your ideals and your value-add systems into checklist that can easily be inspected on a daily basis by the management staff or you.

**Use the rest of this page to write out the step-by-step process needed to provide your product and services to the *Mass-Audience*.

If you need help building a duplicatable and scalable process for your business, you are not alone. We worked with one major national appliance store that had great products but nothing in the way of checklists and operational systems to run things effectively on the store level. Simply by equipping their team with the right tools, they made huge improvements and increases in revenue within the first two months. If you need more information about our business coaching sessions contact us today by going to **www.MakeYourLifeEpic.com or give us a call today at 918-851-6920. Creating a "workflow" (the duplicatable and scalable process for your business) can be over-whelming. The best book / resource for learning how to build a work-flow that works is found within the book entitled, *The E-myth Revisited* by Michael Gerber.

*****

Chapter 5:
Quality Control

If it is not measurable it is not manageable.

"Good management consists in showing average people how to do the work of superior people." - John D. Rockefeller (Oil Tycoon, world's richest man during his time)

There have been countless books written entirely about quality control and management; however, it all comes down to six simple concepts and one incredible man at the end of the day.

Rule #1: If you can't measure it, you can't manage it

If you want your people to do something, you have to find a way to make their results quantifiable or their reasons for not producing the results will always be justifiable. If you want them to market more, what is the specific number of prospects you want them to reach? If you want them to "try harder to improve quality," as a percentage they must know how many errors they are currently making. If your team needs to "be on time more," then you must be able to explain to them what percentage of the time they are currently late. When it gets right down to it, you have to measure everything that you want to ever manage. Find a way to quantify everything that you want done. Have your people track their results and their progress and hold them accountable.

Rule #2: Inspect what you want people respect

If you want your team to respect anything you say and any objectives that you intend on achieving, you must be relentless with your follow-up. Sam Walton was known for his "relentless follow-up." He was known for writing something down into the little notepad he always carried around and following up with people relentlessly people over and over until their task had been completed. John D. Rockefeller was also famous for writing down the action steps and tasks that needed to be done into the little notepad he always carried around. Over time people began to fear just the very image of him and his little notebook because it meant he was going to be following up with you on something that you had forgotten to do. These men became the titans of their industries and they were famous for their relentless follow up. Shouldn't you too be famous for your relentless tenacity about getting things done? You must demand that your direct reports keep a tangible to-do-list. Your people must know that you and your leadership team is going to follow-up on everything. Your people must know that you are going to survey your clients. Your people must know that the boss can come down at any time. If you actually expect your team to do anything you have to inspect everything.

Rule #3: Differentiation

Jack Welch, the greatest C.E.O. of all time and the wizard of modern management came up with this system, and it works.

Essentially his belief is that in every group of people, there are A, B, and C players.

Your A players go over and above and are always looking for constructive criticism. They bring a passion to work every day and they are your top 10% of employees. These people work with energy. These people execute plans and get things done no matter what. These people have an edge to them; they don't mind irritating C players to get something done. These people are your all-stars.

Your B players are needed to achieve your company's goals. They are consistent and they are on-time. They rarely show up early and almost never stay late. They have passion on occasion, but more than anything, they are consistent. You need these people do get things done, because they make up 80% of your workforce, but these people do not have the passion, drive, and ambition that A players have. You can't grow an organization comprised of only B players. Your goal should be to push and encourage your B players to become A players. But this all starts with YOU RECOGNIZING WHO IS AN A PLAYER, WHO IS A B PLAYER and WHO IS A C PLAYER. You must be candid with yourself and with your team about everyone's overall job performance. Does this force you to judge people? Absolutely it does.

My friend once you start being candid with yourself and your team you will discover that your C players are chronically late, tired, frustrated, down, wore-out, demotivated, etc... These people are always "running late because of traffic." These people are always asking "can you remind me next time so I won't forget." These people love saying, "I've never really done that before, and I don't think that is really my job." These people have no passion for life and their job. These people complain and destroy morale. These people are sarcastic and they are negative. These people cannot be pushed to greatness. In fact these people get defensive when presented with constructive criticism. These people make up the bottom 10% of your workforce and they must be fired before clients fire you. As Sam Walton (the founder of Wal-Mart) put it, "There is only one boss. The customer. And he can fire everybody in the company from the chairman on down, simply by spending his money somewhere else." You must fire these people as soon as possible.

Jack Welch believes that every employee should be graded on an A, B, and C level, and that everyone should know where they rank in the company. He believed that every company needs to be honest with their employees at all times about where they stand in the company. He believed that all C players should be fired as soon as you can, as long as they know where they stood and as long as they were given the opportunity to improve. I agree with Jack Welch. This system works.

However, the key to making this system work is in the praising of your A players, the pushing of the B players (to improve), and the firing of the C players (who refuse to get things done).

If you would like for our team to send you an example of what a good employee ranking system and evaluation sheet looks like, visit our website today at **www.MakeYourLifeEpic.com and request this information. For more information about Jack Welch's system, purchase his best-selling book, *Winning*.

Rule #4: Candor Is King

If you want to be an effective manager you are going to have to be candid. Jack Welch the former C.E.O. of General Electric was famous for saying, "be candid with everyone." This sounds simple enough, but I sincerely believe that less than 10% of all companies use candor on a daily basis with themselves and their employees. Candor is the art of stating the realities of job performance to your people without sugar-coating and diminishing the cold hard facts. When you are 100% candid, your people can trust you all the time, because they know that you are telling them the good and the bad. When you only tell people good, over time it diminishes the meaning of a "good job."

In fact most managers that don't use candor tell everyone that they are doing a "good job." However, the harsh reality of business is that you either "did or did not do something." You either "got the deal or you didn't get the deal." You either "made the client happy" or the client "is not pleased". Learn to stop sugar coating things in meetings with your team. Learn to tell them how they did in a candid and truthful way.

Walt Disney, Oprah and the big achievers in human history didn't achieve greatness by consistently lowering their standards to meet the low life and business expectations of those around them. If your employees want to smoke have them smoke in the back by the trash dumpsters so that customers will not see them. Will this irritate them? Yes. Does the Kohl's retail store make their employees go smoke by the smelly trash dumpsters? Yes they do. If you want to demand that your employees must say, "my pleasure" to every client who asks them for something this initially will not go over well. Some employees will forget. Some employees won't want to do it. However, do Chik-Fil-A franchise owners insist that their employees must say, "my pleasure?" Yes they do. Does it irritate their employees? Yes, it does. My friend, don't lower your standards.

You must fight for your success. You must demand that you and others meet the high expectations and ideals your customers want. People trust candid people, and trust helps to build solid friendships. In fact, political personality and super-reporter Bill O'Reilly said it best when he said, "If you have good friends keep them. If you don't have good friends, get them. True friendship, a rare gift, is never taken lightly. Your friends will tell you the truth about yourself, and not charge you $200 an hour. They will tell you the truth but they will stick by you when the rest of the world turns away."

When your sales numbers come in, when the customer satisfaction surveys come in, or when you go to the bank to make your weekly deposits you will be forced to confront the harsh realities of how people actually did. Don't sugar-coat everything you say with "false kindness," because eventually you will have to be frank with your people. And nothing feels worse than having to fire someone because of their subpar job performance after you have been telling them they have been doing "good job" for the past two years.

Rule #5: Problems, Solutions, Action Steps, Accountability, Deadlines & Knowing Your Numbers

As the "entrepreneur, visionary, leader and founder" of your company, you are going to have to lead a lot of meetings. When you lead these meetings, you had better have a coherent format to get things done. You must be able to energize your team or your staff is going to fall asleep if they can't find a way to text back and forth with their buddies about fantasy football without getting caught. The format for these meetings is simple, yet profound.

A. Problems - What is the "root" of the problems from last week? What are the issues?

B. Solutions - What are some viable ways to actually solve these problems?

C. Action Steps - What are the specific action steps we must take to solve these problems?

D. Accountability – Who SPECIFICALLY is assigned to getting these tasks done? Whose INDIVIDUAL responsibility is it? Teams are evil. Groups are bad. Who is the individual who is going to be held accountable for getting the problems solved and getting things done on time.

E. Deadlines - You must assign a deadline for everything, or nothing will get done. The smarter people are, the better they become about justifying things. Make sure you hold your people accountable to hitting their deadlines every time.

F. Knowing Your Numbers - You and your team must know your numbers. You must manage by the numbers only. How many did you sell? What was your closing percentage? What is your conversion percentage? What percentage of your clientele is happy? What percentage of your clientele is not happy? How many appointments did your sales team go on? How much did you spend on food last month? How much were your credit card fees this month? Don't allow people to say things like, "the numbers were pretty good" or "we had around fifty."

Remember, if you can't measure it you can't manage it. And if you can't quantify it, your weakest employees will justify it.

Rule #5: Merit-based pay will save the day

If you are going to systematically grow and systematically keep your best people, you are going to have to implement a system of merit-based pay. You have to reward the best job performances with the best pay. If Trevor, Kevin, Suzanne, Gus, Larry, Uncle Lewis, Clark, George, Kramer, and Raymond all go out to work for you this week, two people are going to do an incredible job, seven people will do what they are supposed to do only, and one person will do an awful job. Let's meet your team.

A. George and Kramer (Your "A Players") - These people will actually show up early and stay late. They will do their job and then they will submit a report on how to make the company better and how to better wow your clients, all without additional compensation. These people show up to work dressing better than the dress-code minimum standards because of personal pride. These two people seem to have a glimmer in their eyes as if they know that this job is just one more step on their road to greatness. These people speak positively and think positively. They are future and solution focused. You need these people and you need to give them a bonus and they need to make 20% more than everyone else so that others can know how much you value their decisions to consistently "go the extra mile."

B. Trevor, Kevi, Suzanne, Gus, Larry, Clark, and Raymond (Your "B Players") - These seven people just do their jobs as described in your operations manual. These people show up at 8:59 A.M. and they work right up until their lunch break. They would never work through lunch to get something done like George and Kramer, but they do get back to work faithfully when then assigned lunch break is over. These guys and gals don't ever really cause problems. Occasionally, Trevor gets motivated to achieve, but it usually only lasts for the two days immediately following his attendance of a motivational conference. Occasionally, these guys show their frustration for Uncle Lewis not doing his job or management hinting about how they should try to work harder. They sometimes say, "That's not my job" and "I'm not getting paid to do that." These people are dependable, honest, and they make-up the majority of your workforce. You need these people. You need to give these guys an annual bonus for their dependability and loyalty, however you must make sure that they make 20% less than George and Kramer. You must also make sure that they know why George and Kramer make more than they do. They must know what kinds of things they must do to make as much as George and Kramer.

C. Uncle Lewis (Your "C Players") -This guy will not care and will do a terrible job. This person will blame "lack of training," or "outside circumstances." This person either "got caught in traffic" or "couldn't do their job because someone else didn't do theirs." This person gets more "flat tires" on an annual basis than anyone else in the entire world and we are counting military Humvee operators. Uncle Lewis lives with his "new girl" at her place because he's "trying to get away from all that baby's mamma drama until it dies down a bit." When you call Uncle Lewis you will have to call his "girl's call for a while" until he "gets his turned back on because the phone company messed up and didn't process his payment just right." When this arrives to work 30 minutes late, this person works with a scowl. This person is chronically tired and loves to up their Facebook status during work. This person is "married to a terrible person" and "you just wouldn't understand." This person "wants to know if they can leave a few minutes early." This person seems to "feel" that this job, like all jobs will lead them nowhere, so they walk slowly. You don't need this person and you need to fire him. This person needs to be fired quickly and everyone needs to know why they were fired, so that the news of their firing spreads throughout the organization. Everyone in your company must know that this type of behavior is simply not acceptable.

Quick Rules for Implementing a Merit-Based Pay System:

1) Reward great work with great pay. Celebrate their success publically. Treat your "A-Players" like all-stars.

2) Reward your "B-Players" with awards for their loyalty and their dependability, but make sure they make 20% less than your "A-Players."

3) Reward "C-Players" and terrible work with quick firings. Publically share what behavior is unacceptable and what work will not be tolerated. News of your high expectations will spread faster than you can possibly talk.

4) Use numbers to determine who does great work and who does not. Survey your clients, measure their satisfaction, find a way to quantify how well your people are doing. If you can't measure it, you cannot manage it fairly.

Once you create a culture where everyone knows where they clearly stand in the organization you will begin to experience huge boosts in morale, quality and ultimately profitability. Most people, with the exception of your "C-Players" want to do a great job and they want to wow their bosses. They want to get promoted and they want to be acknowledged. Ultimately a culture of candor will allow you throw an elbow when needed, while giving the pat on the back when your team wins. Without candor, false-kindness will prevail and organization's quality, morale and revenues will fall.

**If you are serious about implementing the winning management systems you are going to need some good software or at the very least you are going to need to create a nice and orderly system of integrated spread sheets for tracking the overall ranking of your staff. If the thought of building and initially setting up these management systems freaks you out, we can help you. Visit www.MakeYourLifeEpic.com or give us a call at the office today at (918) 851-6920.

*****

Bonus Profound Truth: Edge

You must do the right thing, even if it's unpopular or your business will fail.

"Great spirits have always encountered violent opposition from mediocre minds." - Albert Einstein

If you are going to succeed as an entrepreneur you are going to have to be more tenacious than the nay-sayers, the excuse makers, and the doubters who are in and outside of your business. You are going to have to be incredibly firm in your convictions and you are going to have to be uncompromising with your quality standards because your customers will be whether you are or not. If you are so worried and preoccupied about the feelings of everyone except your customer, you are going to fail. You are going to have to hire and fire people. Your great ideas *Will Consistently Encounter Violent Opposition From Mediocre Minds.* Mediocre people produce mediocre products and service and mediocre bosses keep them around. If you are going to make it to the top, you must have an *Edge* to you. You must make the big decisions and the tough choices. As an entrepreneur, you can delegate everything except the decision making. Again, this *Nugget Is So Profound It Is Worth Retyping. As An Entrepreneur, You Can Delegate Everything, Except The Decision Making.* You are going to have to become comfortable with making the right decision every time, even if it is not the popular decision.

To be a top level entrepreneur you are going to have to be like a sword. A sword is neither bad nor good. A sword is a tool. It can be used to cut things, to fight enemies, to make Kabobs, to use as decoration, etc.... Just like a sword, on occasion you are going to have to kill enemies and on occasion you are going to have to be used as decoration. Be prepared for this. Because when the time comes, you must be ready to make those *Tough Decisions*, you are going to have to have a sharp edge if you are going to be an effective sword and not just a useless tool.

*****

Bonus Profound Truth: Execute

You and your business get paid for what problems you solve, not for what problems you intend on solving.

"Be a yardstick of quality. Some people aren't used to an environment where excellence is expected." - Steve Jobs (Founder of Apple)

One of things that I love about business is the white and black, cut and dry, you did it or you didn't do it aspect of it. When your business and your team knock out projects on time, and consistently deliver on your promises, you will build a solid reputation for yourself and your company and *You Will Be Able To Charge More Money.* If your company consistently runs behind and consistently runs over deadlines you will develop a poor reputation and *You Will Have To Charge Less Money.* Overtime, you will basically be exchanging your reputation for compensation. So I ask you, how's your reputation right now? Do people see you as the person who dresses well, shows up early, and delivers projects on time (if not early)? The late great Andrew Carnegie (one of America's wealthiest men of all time) once wrote, "As I grow older, I pay less attention to what men say. I just watch what they do."

Right now, *Before Your Business Gets Huge*, you must decide what your company's reputation will be. Will your company be the next Lexus? Will your company be the next Starbucks? Will your company be known for its relentless pursuit of perfection or will your company be known for its relentless justification of imperfection? Once you have determined how you want your company to be perceived and viewed, it is now time to turn these ideals into reality. To turn these ideals into reality you are going to have to hire people that execute and actually produce results. In a small and growing business there is absolutely zero room for justifiers. In a small and growing business everyone must execute. Everyone must deliver. Demand that your team executes your exacting standards. Don't tolerate mediocrity. Measure your team's results and reward those who execute your game plan. Take a moment now and write out a brief description of what your company's product standards will be and how you plan on rewarding those who execute your plans and turn your quality standards into reality:

_____

_____

_____

_____

_____

**Note: People that execute and get things done are rare. It is going to take relentless follow-up, recruiting, training, hiring and firing to build a team that delivers results. Don't think you are going to build a Super Bowl winning football team without cutting some players. Don't be so compassionate with your underperforming employees that customers begin to passionately leave you. Prune your business tree of those that simply do not deliver on what they promise you and your customers.

*****

Chapter 6:
Spidering

Systematic follow-up and the art of turning one deal (sale) into three deals.

"If you do build a great experience, customers tell each other about that. Word of mouth is very powerful." - Jeff Bezos

In order to grow your business quickly and exponentially you must learn to become effective at the process I call "Spidering." If you spent an afternoon watching spiders doing their thing you would be one weird human, however you would also learn a thing or two about business from them. Spiders don't make webs out of one piece of spider string. Spiders spread their webs out, and overtime they become more and more intricate, because these guys are focused on catching other bugs in their web (net). Spiders might not be able to memorize the Periodic Table, but they do understand that they are going to need a bigger web, if they are going to catch more food. As a business owner or entrepreneur you must come to grips with this right now.

Over the years, I have met numerous bitter, broken and poor entrepreneurs who believe that "my great product should sell itself." This is bogus and this is a good tip on how not to be successful. In order to make *Big Money Now* you must learn this "Spidering" system now. "Spidering" is nothing more than the systematic approach of turning one sell into three sells and one contact into 100 contacts. Listed below you will find my seven rules for effective "Spidering."

Rule #1 - Get the e-mail address, name, phone number, name, and profession of every human you talk with. If someone buys something from you, get their e-mail address. If you meet a business owner at Starbucks, get their e-mail address, name, phone number, and profession. If you meet a human, get their information. Do this every time. You will be amazed by how many deals you will close just buy utilizing automated marketing to people whom you have met.

Rule #2 - Put all the contact information you ever collect into a database (I recommend the ACT! Software or the SalesForce.com software.

Rule #3 - Make it your mission to help your clients solve their problems whether or not your service is the one who can help them or not. If you own a bakery that specializes in wedding cakes, make it your priority to insure that every bride finds a great band, D.J., florist, photographer, etc....Go out of your way to improve the quality of their day by helping them to solve their problems.

Rule #4 - Whenever you give a referral, make sure you follow-up by calling the service provider you referred to tell them about the referral you sent them. You must establish and maintain "top of mind awareness" with each and every one of the service providers you refer. Referrals are like boomerangs.

They will never come back and unless you actually throw them out there to begin with. You must first give a referral, if you ever expect to get one.

Rule #5 - Make it your team's mission to over-deliver, to wow, and to exceed the expectations of every client. Show up early. Bring your clients a little "something extra". Bring your clients joy, exceed their expectations and do something for them that is well above what they expected and your clients simply will not be able to stop talking about you and the great job you did for them. If you simply do what you promised, clients will not talk about you. When was the last time you simply could not stop telling others about how excited you are about the energy provider for your home? When was the last time you referred your trash collection company to a friend because they were "so consistent?"

Rule #6 - Become Facebook friends with all *Satisfied Customers*. After the service has been provided, survey each and every one of your clients via e-mail. If the customer gives your company high marks, you must invite your clients to become Facebook friends. Don't invite people to become your Facebook friends when you 1st meet. They might be psychotic

Rule #7 - You must focus on taking your relationship with every buyer from that of "just a buyer" to that of a "client" and then ultimately that to that of an "apostle" and a "viral fan of the business." This process takes a while but it will be done if you are systematic and diligent with your Spidering efforts.

Rule #8 - Send your clients at least four e-mail newsletters per year. Just like friends, clients can forgot about you if they haven't seen you in a while. There is a strong chance that the buddies and homies that you had back in college are no longer super close with you today. Why is that? You have to stay on the minds of your clients or you will be forgotten.

Rule #9 - Routinely post your company's testimonials and good news via your Facebook page. Clients and potential clients must see that your company is consistently prospering, growing and wowing other clients if they are to remember you when they need you and if they are going to begin virally referring your business.

Rule #10 - Stay aware of contests, business awards, and other public relations opportunities that your company is eligible for. These awards and contests often require testimonials from previous clients, and certified financial records. Make sure your company stays in contention for these awards, and then make sure that you ask your "apostle" and "super happy clients" for their support in providing a testimonial for your company. When people invest their time in a business or organization they naturally begin to become even more loyal to your brand.

Rule #11 - Keep your customer relationships fresh. You must energize your company relationships with over-the-top and memorable customer appreciation parties at regular intervals. You must send out customer surveys, vendor appreciation events, and other events that will give you face time with your clients to tell them "thank you" without attempting to "sell them" anything. Think about the cult of energized customers that Harley Davidson has amassed over the years. Harley customers are always organizing biker rallies, bragging about their motorcycles and promoting the brand because they love the brand. To build a "love" relationship with anyone it requires an investment of quality time and a consistency of interaction. How can you develop these "love relationships" with your customers? What events will you host? What marketing events will you put into your calendar?

Rule #12 - Be the guy (or lady) that mails *Hand-Written* "Thank You Notes" to your clients. When you mail a "thank you" note, you will break out of the "clutter of commerce" almost immediately. People remember "thank you notes" and "personal letters from companies" and they will talk about them.

Rule #13 - Be memorable to your clients. Be the Fitness Boot camp that brings more energy than anybody else. Be the bakery whose cakes are over the top. Be the insurance agent who is hilarious and who always wears a bow-tie. Be the conservative business owner who is always rocking a "faux-hawk" on your head. Be the business that has real "cool" factor associated with it (think of the Apple retail stores). Be professional, yet be *Memorable*. Being professional is not enough. If you are not memorable, you will not be remembered.

**Creating a checklist and a duplicatable system for "spidering" in your business is very important and very uncommon. Countless studies show that time and time again, well over 80% of small businesses fail within their first two years and I would argue that much of this is due to the fact that most small businesses are clueless about how to leverage their existing client base. I certainly once was. If you need help developing an effective "spidering system," I recommend that you would give our office a call so that we can setup a brain-storming session with our team. We've built countless "spidering" (leveraging) systems for companies all over the country and it is incredible to see them work. Getting more business and more referrals from your existing book of business has the power to change everything.

*****

Mind-Expanding Bonus Profound Truth: Public Relations

You must know how to tell your story in a way that is news worthy.

"You have to fake it before you make it." - Lori Montag
(Founder of Zany Bandz & Slap Watch)

When the Beatles landed in New York City in 1964, "Beatle Mania" officially began. As the four band members got off the plane, they were greeted by 3,000 screaming teenagers at the airport. Some were in tears and some were carrying placards with phrases such as "I love you, please stay". Once these young pioneers of rock stepped off of the plane and onto the tarmac of Kennedy Airport, they were instant celebrities! Did these 3,000 fans all happen to know the precise landing time of the Beatles or did someone tell them? Did these fans run out and buy these placards or did someone give them a budget before telling them what to buy and what to write? Did these fans decide to scream at their own prompting or were they coached?

My friends, the beginning of "Beatle Mania" was one of the best examples of P.R. at work in American history. As the Beatles arrived at the United States, the "British Invasion" hype looked as though it would be greeted by ten kids who were vaguely familiar with this British Band and the songs they played. However, employees from the local radio station and the publicists for the Beatles organized and paid a group of teenagers to scream and cheer, thus perpetuating the creation of the atmosphere of hype that began to surround these four young men everywhere they went. How much less excited would America have been if the American news outlets weren't able to show that memorable footage of 3,000 teenagers and adoring fans screaming as they got off the plane? Did the

Beatles become big because they were already big? Or did they become big because they were so good? Only God truly knows, but I know P.R. certainly did not hurt.

Frank Sinatra's publicist team actually paid young teenagers wearing bobbysoxers to scream, cheer and fake actual hysteria as he performed. This began to create the atmosphere of *Hype* and celebrity that would make Frank Sinatra famous. Did Sinatra become famous, because he had screaming fans before he was famous? I think it is worth considering.

People started inquiring about booking me for speaking events within days after I had received the United States Small Business Administration Entrepreneur of the Year award. Was I not smart up until then? Was my success not worth examining before I received this award? Would it have been smart for me to have hired a publicist to share our business accolades with the media earlier? Would it probably have been a good idea for me to get my information into the publications that event coordinators, conference organizers and workshop planners read a long time ago? Would it make sense for you to begin launching a strategic public relations campaign designed to get your business in front of your target audience starting today? But how do you start? Who do you contact? And why would the media be willing to cover you and your business when there are so many other companies out there that have news worthy stories?

A competitor once pointed out that one of our business coaching clients was getting "over-exposed" because she had literally been in nearly every publication in her local market within 1 calendar year. The public relations strategy we developed for her was intense. She was in the newspapers, in the magazines, on the television stations and in the big competitions. Her business more than doubled in size. If you were a competitor would you think she was getting "over-exposed" too? If your business was in the news every 4 weeks and your phone was ringing off the hook with inquiries would that be a bad thing for your business?

One of the businesses that I have invested in is a men's grooming lounge in Tulsa, Oklahoma called the "Elephant In the Room" Men's Grooming Lounge. The business model involves offering hot towel treatments, shampoos, paraffin hand-dips, shoulder massages, hand massages, straight razor shaves, cuts and hair-styling for men. The market was already saturated with hair salons and places for guys to get their haircut. In every market in the country there is a "Super Cuts," or a "Top Cuts" or some dirty place that tries to lure in guys to get their haircut by attracting men with hair stylists dressed in lingerie or something even more revealing. The pricing structures are all very cheap and the industry of men's grooming has essentially become a commodity in most communities.

Because our business model was designed to create an experience we decided to charge significantly more than our competitors. We also decided that we needed to employ some of the PR strategies I am teaching you hear. Within 6 weeks of opening our doors we were featured in the Tulsa World, the Journal Record, the Tulsa Business Journal and the nightly news. We were also contacted about being featured in a prominent high-end local magazine called, Tulsa People. Did the media have nothing else to talk about or did we simply use a strategy that works? Could you use this strategy to quickly grow your business? Absolutely you could. If your product is good and you are willing to follow this system, you can absolutely succeed with PR.

My friend, you must decide right here and now that you are a *Big Deal*. Someday your business is going to make *Big Money*, because starting right now you are going to treat your business, your employees, your clients, and yourself like you are a *Big Deal*. Whenever a peacock is trying to impress another peacock, it will puff its feathers out to look bigger and more beautiful than it is. In nature, when many animals are about to fight, they will puff out their hair to try to scare off a rival. Nature does it and humans do it also. The goal is to look big before you are big, because nothing creates momentum like momentum and nothing inspires confidence and trust like media coverage. Being on the news is big news for your business. During this chapter I am going to teach you how to get in the news, but it only works if you follow this system with tenacity, diligence, and caution. There are only four major networks in most local markets and only fifteen to twenty major publications that cover most industries. You don't want to get a bad reputation amongst the reporters, writers, and news community as being "that guy." You don't want to appear to be an amateur when working with the media. Once you are known as "that guy," it is truly very hard to overcome this problem because the local media consists of a very small group of people. There are probably only four well known weathermen in your local market and eight well known news anchors. If you go around irritating these people, you are in for a long uphill battle. TV personalities tend to stick around a local market for a long time, so your battle will be a long one if go about things the wrong way.

Getting your company featured in the news, in a magazine, on TV, on the radio, in a newspaper, on a news blog, etc....simply involves the following seven step process:

1. Find out who currently covers stories about your market niche / industry, etc....

This process is really as simple as a grabbing a copy of each of your local papers to see which reporters covers each area of the news. Even doing a "Google Search" for your industry plus the name of the local publication you want to research will get the job done. For instance, if I lived in Tulsa and I wanted to get my real estate business covered in the local media I would "Google Search," "Tulsa World + Real Estate Market." This search would soon show that Kevin might write about real estate in my city, while John might be the one who writes about business in my city. Shelly covers the downtown related stories, while Ed covers the news of the weird. Regardless of who covers what, it is absolutely critical that you begin to build a database of the reporters and journalists that cover each area of news for your location media outlets. As you look through the papers, you will soon discover the reporters that write about the industry you are in. You must do this research for every publication that you have an interest of appearing in.

2. Gather the contact information for those that cover your market niche / industry.

Once you have discovered the first and last names of the journalists and members of the media that write about your industry niche for each media outlet, it is time to do some more research. We must now gather their contact information. This is generally very easy to do, because most journalists and reporters publish their contact info freely so that they can be reached by people in their city that might have "an inside scoop" for them. Look on the "contact us" sections of the websites for each company they represent. Call the media outlets over the phone and ask for their contact information.

Discover the pattern with which their e-mail addresses are signed. For example, you might discover that the e-mails for the *Sun Times* all are in the following format: Jill.Smith@SunTimes.com, Naven.Johnson@SunTimes.com, King.Richard@SunTimes.com, etc.... With obvious patterns like this, it does not take a genius to discover what Moses Malone's e-mail address would be: Moses.Malone@SunTimes.com. My friend, you must be resourceful here. You can do it! However, if you can't you need to stop with this entrepreneurship non-sense as soon as possible, because being an entrepreneur is all about being resourceful in a way that would make MacGyver proud (the world's most resourceful man).

3. Build rapport and establish yourself as the expert for your industry with these reporters.

To build sincere rapport with the members of the media that cover your industry niche for the various outlets, I recommend making a quick initial call to them, while following up with a quick hand-written physically mailed note of appreciation for them and the level of quality they bring to their writing. Remember, the members of the media are people too! Ultimately they have goals and dreams, just like you. What are the dreams of a journalist and reporter? What makes these members of the media tick? What gets them excited? As a general rule, I have found that the following character description is true of the overwhelming majority of the members of the media.

The typical member of the media is a four-year graduate from a liberal arts college. They are usually left-leaning (Democrat) in their political leanings. They tend to feel underpaid and overworked. Because they cover the news every day, and because many of them have to come up with a news story that meets their publication's standards every twenty-four hours, most tend to rely heavily upon publicists and P.R. firms for the stories they cover. They are always in a hurry and they are always up against a deadline for getting something "on the air" or "in the news before they go to print." Most have a strong desire to do well in a smaller local market in the hopes that their work will get noticed on a national level which will offer them the opportunity to work for a national media outlet or content provider. Just like you and I, they want to achieve success in their field by getting a "big deal," which for them is a "big story." Help them break a big story and they will love you forever. They take their commitments and promises very seriously. They will never give up their sources and they work very hard to build trust with the local news makers so they can always have the "inside scoop" about what is going on. They need these insiders for the "tips" and "news story ideas" they provide.

Because the profile above is so accurate, the script for your first call to them should really be very similar do this. "Hey is this Pat? Pat, did I catch you right up against a deadline? Okay, well here's the scoop. I do a lot of work in the downtown real estate industry, and I just want you to know that I'm a fan of your work. That article you wrote about the new hotel downtown was great. Well hey, I know you have to run, I just wanted to let you know, I do a lot of work downtown and if you ever need a source for your downtown stories, please don't hesitate to call."

Follow-up this call with the mailing of a hand-written note. let them know how much you enjoy their work. Make sure to include your contact information and your area of expertise, so that they can use you as an expert resource in the future.

4. Develop a marketing / public relations calendar full of events, press conferences, parties, conferences, visually appealing, intriguing, Genius-World-Record-Breaking and other newsworthy events that would be of interest to the journalist's core audience.

Now that you know who covers what, and now that you have established yourself as an expert in your local community it is time for the fun part. You now must develop your twelve-month plan. Remember as Napoleon Hill once wrote, "Reduce your plan to writing. The moment you complete this, you will have definitely given concrete form to the intangible desire." Nothing will happen until you write out this plan and commit to turning it into reality.

You must create a twelve-month P.R. strategy. Your strategy must be filled with innovative ideas that will keep the media talking. The best way to do this is to do a "Google Search" for your industry's name plus the name of a local city (other than the one that you are wanting to work in).

For example, if I was in the wedding industry in Dallas and I wanted to develop a marketing calendar for my Dallas wedding business. I would search for "Miami Wedding Industry, plus the name of the local publication." I would then begin to write down what the articles in Miami were about. I would do this research for each one of the major publications in Miami until I had my twelve ideas based upon what the Miami media actually covered locally in my industry. If the Miami media thought the story was news worth enough to warrant media coverage, there is a strong possibility that my local media will feel the same way about our local story ideas.

My friend, your life will be much easier if you commit to being a "Pirate instead of a pioneer." Sir Isaac Newton said, "If I have seen further than others, it is by standing upon the shoulders of giants." His comments were demonstrating his belief in not-reinventing the wheel every time. If somebody else has done it before you, by all means use their ideas in a new and creative way. Don't feel the need to start from scratch with a completely original idea every time. If you do this, you will need to live for six lifetimes to every get anything done.

5. Write a newsworthy story / "press-release" in a standard format that will appeal to the journalist's core audience.

Over time, journalists have developed a standard formula with which they expect every press-release to appear. Due to the extreme busyness and the dead-line driven nature of today's media, they also expect you to know what this formula is. They expect you to write a catchy headline for them. They expect for you to include the facts that support the details of the story. They expect your press-releases to be news worthy and appropriate for them and their areas of focus.

Doing a simple "Google Search" for a standard press release format will help you to learn the standard format the news media wants your releases in. However, you must never forget that your "press-releases" are being sent to humans, humans like you and me that get flooded with *Spam*, and unwanted e-mails and faxes. Just like with any other form of marketing you must ask yourself, what is my "purple cow" here? What about this press-release will grab the attention of the reporter and the viewers of this media outlet or publication?

6. Submit your "press-release" to the media at the times when they are listening and at intervals that are appropriate.

Nobody gets more bad story ideas and poorly written news ideas than the members of your local media. Thus, their defenses are up, so you must write e-mail subject lines, e-mail bodies and press-releases that get their attention for all the right reasons.

The members of the media expect you to know what times of day are most appropriate for to submit your press-releases. Not knowing this information is not an excuse. You must find out when the best time is to submit your press-releases and when the worst time is. If your local reporter is in a staff meeting and news planning meeting everyday at 10:00 A.M. and they are in the habit of checking their e-mail for news story ideas right before this meeting each day, it might make sense to always send them news stories at 9:50 A.M. You must find out the time of day when each of these reporters and members of the media are the most receptive to news story ideas. You do not want to be "that guy" who always calls them right when they are in the process of finalizing an article that must "go to print" in the next ten minutes.

7. After you have sent the press-release, you must follow-up with a "quick call" to verify that press-release has been received without irritating anyone.

Use this script when placing your follow-up call to keep this call from going badly, "Hey is this Jim? Jim, are you up against a hard deadline? Well hey, here is the scoop... I just sent you an article about how the State of Texas will benefit from the forty-two graphic design jobs that are being created in downtown Dallas by the good folks at Clay & Associates. Did you receive the fax and e-mail I sent you? As always, if you have any questions, just let me know."

Be prepared to talk fast to think fast and to answer any questions they may have about the validity of your story, your sources and your ideas. Understand that the very nature of a reporter's job forces them to be alarmingly direct and frank. They must quickly discern between fact or fiction and newsworthy or not newsworthy. They simply, must move quickly if they are going to hit their deadlines. And they will hit their deadlines or they will be dead.

8. Follow-up on features, news articles or TV segments with a compliment, and hand-written "thank you notes."

The overwhelming majority of the members of the media have very high-integrity and huge passion for what they do, because they certainly do not get paid enough to be in it just for the money. Every time a reporter or member of the media writes a story about something, they are putting their neck out there. Get in the habit of writing a handwritten note to thank them for their gracious article and the time they allotted in covering the story. Sincerely compliment the areas of the feature piece that you liked the most then send this physical letter to them in the mail A.S.A.P. Build relationships with these people and is well. Irritate this people and you will have problems.

**If you feel like you need someone to help you create a winning PR strategy call our office today. We've produced effective PR strategies for companies of all types. Whether you are working with in real estate company, a bakery, a men's styling salon, a church, a non-profit or a mortgage company you need effective PR to win customers. For additional information on how to write an effective press-release in an acceptable format read *Guerilla P.R. 2.0* by Michael Levine.

Get this book and use it as a reference. It's best PR book ever written! If you would like to hire a P.R. firm to handle this madness for you, we can also recommend the best P.R. firm for you. Just give us a call or visit us online at: **www.MakeYourLifeEpic.com**.

Chapter 7:
Accounting

It's not about how much you make, it's about how much you keep.

"No.1: Never lose money. Rule No.2: Never forget rule No.1."
- Warren Buffett

When you start a business you must do your due diligence to account for every dime that must be spent to make a transaction happen. If are not diligent about this, you will find yourself working seventeen-hour days without making a profit. Hypothetically, it is very possible to bring in large amount of gross revenue (gross revenue is the initial amount of money you bring in before expenses), while netting very little. And if you do a ton of work, but profit very little, you are going to be in a world of hurt when it comes to pay day. When you do your costing for your business, you must observe my seven rules and you will be fine.

Rule #1: Pay yourself first

Make sure you pay yourself first. On every transaction, make sure you slice off an amount to pay yourself. If you own a car dealership, every time a car is sold make sure you get paid something. You must pay yourself first.

Rule #2: Produce a 20% profit

After each service or product is delivered make sure that you have at least a 20% profit margin remaining. If your business is not making at least a 20% profit margin, banks and investors will be very hesitant to lend you money.

Rule #3: Use a variable pay method when possible

According to the Small Business Administration, well over 85% of all the jobs created in the United States are created by small business owner. And having spent massive amounts of time working as a consultant / speaker and trainer with thousands of small business owners, it is apparent that most small business owners do not have huge amounts of startup capital. Thus, protecting your initial startup capital is super important. Paying your team on a variable based pay out system will make this possible. Pay your initial team on a commission only basis if possible. Don't pay any money out, unless money comes in. This system is the best. Offer huge commissions and big incentives, but simply refuse to pay any money out unless money comes in. Essentially you are telling your team, "you will get paid generously for what you do, and nothing for what you only intend on doing."

Rule #4: Don't forget to account for the small stuff

You must account for the small stuff. An American politician and Senator, Everett Dirksen, once said, "A billion here, a billion there, and pretty soon you're talking real money." *Wow*, those guys are out of touch. However, what I am talking about is:

A. Don't forget to account for credit card processing fees (when 3% of your revenue disappears on every transaction it adds up quickly).

B. Don't forget to account for payroll tax. Because all of the payroll tax software programs, "automatically deduct everything from your account" to simplify things, most American business people have no idea, how much money they are actually paying for this.

C. Don't forget to account for insurance. My least favorite expense is insurance. Whenever you are buying insurance you are buying a piece of paper and a promise, however having good insurance has been shown to help entrepreneurs sleep better. I've been in business since I was fifteen and I can tell you that something bad is going to happen. To quote Kirk Fryer (District Manager) of Farmer's Insurance, "Make sure you have a bad day, and not a bad life."

D. Don't forget to account for refunds. Sure, you are a genius and you will never have to give refunds, but every other company will. Refunds are going to happen, either because a customer is nuts, or because one of your employees decided to smoke pot before his last shift.

E. Don't forget to account for theft. Stuff is going to get stolen. As our country drifts farther and farther from our founding ideals, morals and values, more and more people are justifying their behavior based on their "situational morality". "Situational morality" is becoming a big part of our lives. Basically, person A is hungry. Person A takes your lunch and doesn't feel bad about it. This makes me want to punch a Koala when I hear it or type it, but it is going to happen. Account for that stuff.

F. Don't forget to account for banking fees. Although it might seem strange, banks are in business to make money. They are constantly coming up with more and more ways to take your money by offering "better service." They'll say, "We will even come to your office to pick up your checks, so you don't have to leave your office!" And for a fee, you could also probably get a guy in your office to glue his nipple to a desk. As convenient as it may sound, those fees add up.

G. Don't forget to account for shipping and handling. It costs money to get items from A to B. Thus, as you put together your spread sheets and as you organize your initial startup costs, you must factor in the costs of shipping and handling. It adds up quickly and if you don't factor it in, as an owner you will never get paid.

H. Don't forget to factor in the "embedded costs" of hiring every employee. I have seen some pro-formas and costing sheets that simply factor in the hourly amount that an employee costs a company, but this is not accurate. Every employee other than Chuck Norris must be managed, and that costs money. Every employee must work somewhere, and a lease or the purchase of a building costs money.

Every employee must have a computer, an internet connection, and phone, this costs money. Every employee must have access to a restroom, this costs money. Just make sure you list all of the costs associated with bringing on an employee.

I. Don't forget any costs. Go through your costing sheet fifty times if you have to, but do not forget any costs, or your business life will quickly be in utter ruin and your demise will happen shortly (that sounded threatening).

Rule #5: No one wants to work for a poor boss.

My friend, it is absolutely essential that you pay yourself more than everybody else who works for you, because you are the boss. You are risking your savings, your time (which is your life), your energy, and everything you have to start a business. Don't feel guilty for paying yourself well for a job well done.

Rule #6: Use merit-based pay to reward "great work" with "great pay."

"Good is the enemy of great" - Jim Collins

It is absolutely important that you allow for great bonuses and great pay for "great work". Survey every client. Measure everything so that you can give generous bonuses for those that are really producing "great results". Don't give bonuses for "working hard". Give bonuses for "great results". Survey your client and give bonuses to your team members who *Wow* the clients time and time again. Make a show about it. Honor them publicly. Everyone in your company should know who does great work and who does good work. Everyone must know that you give bonuses only for "great work".

For more information on creating and implementing a merit-based pay system read and apply the principles found in *The Service Profit Chain* by James L. Heskett. If you are stumped, visit **www.MakeYourLifeEpic.com and send us a message. We will help you do this.

Rule #7: Make sure you are achieving your financial goals

After adding up all of your costs, if you don't make enough money on a "per product / service basis" to achieve your goals, adjust your numbers. Keep adjusting your numbers until you are making enough money to make it worth it. Don't start this business just because you "already have a degree in this area" or because "your father was in this industry." You have to make money to make it worth it. Years ago I worked with the owner of an apparel business. After doing the math we soon discovered that after paying for all the expenses, he only average $2 per item of profit. Much to his amazement, we both discovered that his business was not even worth doing if the variables stayed the same. At the time he was killing himself working 12 hours days just to make 500 shirts per week. If he ever wanted to achieve his financial goals he was going to have to sell 2,500 shirts per week. Based on the business model that he wanted to stick with, he would have to work 60 hour days to achieve his goal or he would have to hire someone else in which case he would only be profiting about 25 cents per sold shirt if there were no printing errors. Something had to change.

I once worked with a cupcake business that sold $2 cupcakes. This company was turning down $700 and $1,000 transactions just to keep up with the production demands caused by those freakin' $2 cupcakes. The $700 and $1,000 transactions had a 50% profit margin and the cupcakes had a 20% profit margin. The large ticket items took 4 hours each to produce. The small ticket items took all day to produce. For this person to achieve their goals, something had to change.

My friend don't become married to business model, become married to achieving your financial goals. Don't continue selling unprofitable items just because you've always done it that way. THINK BIG.

Rule #8: Automate and outsource when possible

If you can automate each transaction with an online shopping cart, do it. If you can outsource or automate any part of your business do it. Automated shopping carts never show up late, they don't "get tired because they got into a fight with their girlfriend," etc.... You are in business to make money. Stay focused.

If you need help creating a detailed costing sheet looks like contact us by visiting the site at **www.MakeYourLifeEpic.com. If the very thought of "accounting" makes your brain explode, please contact our team at (918) 851-6920. After years of business coaching we have developed a network of nation-wide accounting professionals that we would be happy to recommend.

*****

Bonus Profound Truth:
Budget Mechanisms - Keeping costs down and quality up.

"Rule No. 1: Never Lose Money. Rule No. 2: Never Forget Rule No. 1." - Warren Buffett

My friend, you are in business to make enough money, to turn your dreams into realities. Thus, if you can't balance your business budget you are going to be in trouble. Although it might seem basic, you need to mentally marinate on Warren Buffett's investing rules, "Rule No. 1: Never Lose Money. Rule No. 2: Never Forget Rule No. 1." You must keep this thought firmly implanted in the forefront of your brain as you grow your business. After having spent many years consulting businesses and running my own companies, I have determined that there are really only "Five Moves" for business budgeting that work consistently. It's true, Michael Jordan had countless "moves" that made him famous as a basketball player, but at the end of the day it was his go to moves that made him famous and so successful. Michael could "slam dunk." Michael could do the "fade away mid-range jump shot." Michael could do the "cross-over dribble." Michael could shoot the "three-pointer" when he needed to. And Michael would also knock down these "free throws" when you fouled him. My friend, don't read seven business books on budgeting. Just master these moves and you will be ahead the game, and your budgeting problems will be solved.

Move #1: Use A Variable Based Pay on Every Aspect of Your Business If Possible

When starting out and looking to grow, pay everyone based on a percentage of the revenue that comes into the business. Share the pain and share the gain with your people. If your sales are down then everyone's pay should be down. This form of payment forces everyone to care about the overall health of the company. This pay mechanism forces people in different departments to have conversations that sound like, "Hey Mary, why can't your sales guys sell anything? We really need to get those numbers higher for everybody. Is there anything I can do to help?" If you don't have this type of payment system in place, you will hear conversations like, "Hey Mary. I don't work in sales, so quit trying to bring me into your mess. That area is not my job!'

Move #2: Keep as Much Cash on Hand as Possible

Cash is king. Although you can borrow against your receivables, cash is king. Although, you might have a great looking spread sheet because your fancy "accrual basis accounting system," if you don't have cash the game is over. Do everything in your power to only spend money when you absolutely have to. To not get seduced into buying the latest "tech gadget" because a lazy person on your staff thinks it is cool. Don't be seduced into buying more "pens and paper" every week because the "creative people" think it would be nice. Only buy things that will help you make more money.

If you are like most entrepreneurs, you are going to have all of your savings, and most of your time and energy invested into your business. The last thing you ever want to do is to get stuck with bills to pay and no money in the bank. You must be beyond vigilant about watching your money. You must be a "maniac of money management". Be intense about managing your money and when possible be the one who personally signs the majority of the checks. Something special happens when you are the one writing the checks. I call this the system of "checks and balances."

As the owner, you will generally find yourself asking profound questions like, "do we really need to buy this?" When you delegate the checking writing too early, you run the risk of someone saying, "Well it's not my money, I'm just the one paying the bills."

Move #3: Each Month Monitor Your Bank Statements, And Watch them like a Hawk

I realize that hawks don't generally watch bank statements, but you get the point. Each month you must look at the money that came in and the money that went out. If the money that came in is less than the money that went out, you have a problem. Don't bury your head in receipts trying to find "the one thing that is really killing you." Look at your bank statement, to see if you are trending up or trending downward in the bank account. Once you know where you are going you can then refer to your "costing sheet" we discussed earlier. You will need to make sure that everything you are buying for your business is being accounting for on your costing sheet. If new costs are added to your business there had better be new revenue coming into offset these expenses.

Move #4: Live Cheap

When you start your business, you must realize that once you run out of cash, the game is over for you and your business. You must constantly check and double check to make sure that you are keeping your costs low. I love entrepreneurship. I love the possibilities, the success and the challenges, but I would be doing you a disservice if I did not dwell on the importance of living cheap when you are starting or growing a business. You can't live in the *Huge* house and drive the *Ultra Nice* car while traveling to the *Best* vacation spots until your business is booming. You don't have to look like you are homeless, but you are going to have to be wise and frugal with your money. When my wife and I were first married, we lived without air conditioning for that first hot and steamy year of marriage. We literally had to choose between air conditioning and advertising for our young business. We chose to advertise. Once the money started to come in we again had to choose between nice cars or new equipment for the business. I think no one really explains this concept better than Dave Ramsey (the personal finance guru who has helped millions). When Dave said, "If you will live like no one else, later you can live like no one else." I think he hit it on the head. My friend, what are willing to live without for the short term so that you can make *Big* money in the long-term?

Move #5: Avoid Business Models That Pay You Later

Business models that involve paying you later are not good. I used to own a party rental business that involved us getting paid 60 days after we had rendered the service and this was not good. I coached with some clients that own staffing businesses where it is totally normal for them to not get paid for 60 days until after they have rendered service and this is not good. I've consulted with construction businesses that did not get paid until 6 months after the house was built and this is not good. In all three of these business models where the company was forced to wait significant amounts of time to collect payment after the service has been rendered financial problems were always looming. Unless you start out with a considerable amount of money in the bank when you start, I would strongly recommend avoid business models that leave you waiting on payment. I know of dozens of examples where the business owners nearly lost it all when a big client decided to withhold payment for months after the service was rendered.

Finding potential clients, marketing to them, selling them something and then delivering on your promises is hard enough. I can't stand business models that require you and I to go and hunt down the "receivables" after we have already rendered service. In my opinion, doing this is stupid. I'm sure that there are people out there that enjoy hunting down their money after they have already rendered service but I am not one of them. If you are going to spend your time hunting down money that is owed, I recommend that you just set up a debt collection service instead, it's more lucrative and you don't have to mess with the marketing, selling, and service delivering stuff.

In all sincerity the debt-collection business can be a profitable because very few people know how to do it and have actually do it. My friend, guard your time, and guard your money. Don't set up a business model that requires you to spend 50% of your time drumming up new business and 50% of your time collecting the balance owed to you.

*****

Chapter 8:
Human Resources

The ultimate throttle on your businesses is determined by the quality of the people that you are able to attract and keep.

"I've been blessed to find people who are smarter than I am, and they help me to execute the vision I have." - Russell Simmons (Founder of Def Jam, Def Comedy Jam, Phat Farm, revered as one of the founders of Hip Hop)

To build a great company you are going to have to attract great people to work with you and *Great People Will Only Be Attracted To Great Big Visions* Carried Out By Leadership That Inspires Confidence. Mentally marinate on that for a second... Great people will only be attracted to *Great Big Visions*. What is your vision? Are you capable of inspiring others to join forces with you? When I started my wedding entertainment business, it was just me. That's all it was, it was just me. Me and myself and I. Why would anyone with a sound mind want to come and work for me when I was nineteen? Why would anyone follow a nineteen year old anywhere? When you start talking about finances, you start talking about how people feed their families and you start talking about how people provide for their families. When you start talking about business and finances, you start talking about the leading cause of divorce. My friend, here is the brutal truth and reality. Nobody is going to want to join forces with you unless you have a big vision, an unbelievable reputation, uncompromising standards and the best work ethic around. You must inspire confidence. You must come to terms with the fact that all successes and failures associated with your business are caused by you. Years ago I worked with a gentlemen who claimed that his business could not grow because there wasn't enough good people out there. He said his financial challenges were caused by not having a good staff. Talking like that is insane if your goal is to achieve financial success.

You have to take ownership of the situation that you are in, because must become the kind of person that "great people will follow." Great people will not follow someone who is unable to take responsibility for their life. Great people are not going to waste their time working for someone who has a small vision, a poor reputation, poor standards and a crappy work ethic.

However, since you bought this book, we can assume that you are a person people would follow. And since you are a person people would follow, let me describe for you the six qualities you are looking for in your people. Remember, you can train nearly any person how to do any skill, but you can't train any great talent how to be a great person. Hire personality, train the skill.

1) Great attitude - Does the job applicant possess alacrity (a brisk and cheerful readiness)? Are they trainable? Are they

excited about life and are they enthusiastic about coming to work every day?

2) Expectations - Does the job applicant have a big vision for their own personal life or are they just happy to be alive? Are they aiming high with their life? Does this person expect to be a millionaire someday? Are they are shooting star or are they a bottom feeder?

3) Edge - Can this job applicant make right decision even when it irritates the mediocre minds around them? Does this person value getting things done more than being well-liked by everyone? If your candidate can't do this, they are not right for your business. But, they can always get a job at a petting zoo.

4) Energy - Is this person capable of bringing passion to their job every day? Will this person show up ready to go every day or does this person wake up just moments before they are supposed to be at work? Does this person have the ability to stay fired up, or this person going to require you to reset them all the time like an old school egg-timer?

5) Execution - Does this new recruit have the ability to get things done? Will this person use some MacGyver technology if needed to get things done, or will this person be great at making excuses. Will this person just "figure it out" or will this person ask, "How do I use Google? What should I type in?"

6) Energize - Will this person energize those around them on the job or will they suck the energy right out of the room like a black hole? Will this person lead by example and act like the Joe Montana or Tom Brady of your office? Will this person set the standard and hold themselves and others accountable to meeting your expectations or will this person say, "It's not my job to inspire everybody else."

The Job Interview:

If you are going to have a productive hiring and firing process, you are going to have to develop a standard format for your job interviewing. Just like a great comedy routine, and an Oscar-winning performance or type of performance "that is done masterfully," your job interview must be done the same every time. You must not be random in the way you interview your candidates. During your interview should follow the following outline every time:

1) Collect the Crap - Each state has its different rules, but make sure you comply with them. Don't lose everything you have worked for just because you're acting dumb. Get this stuff filled out!

A. Make an application, or use a state provided form to have your candidate officially apply for your job. You want to make sure that you do collect the following pieces of information from every human you decide to hire regardless of what state you live in.

    1. Legal name

    2. Two phone numbers

    3. E-mail address

    4. Home address

    5. Mailing address

    6. Five personal references

    7. Social security number

8. Criminal history disclosure

9. Signed employee agreement (stating how you hire and fire)

10. Their five-year goals

11. Their one-year goals

12. Their education history / background

13. Their job history / career history / resume

B. Make sure you collect the physical documentation you need.

1. Get a copy of their driver's license.

2. Get a copy of another form of identification.

1) Rapport - Get the candidate to like and trust you

A. Script out questions you will use to find common ground with the candidate.

B. Example: "Tell me what you have been doing for the past year?" "Tell me about your educational background and what you like doing when you are not working?"

2) Needs - Find out about the candidates life goals

A. Script out the questions you will use to determine the candidates life goals.

B. Example, "Where do you see yourself in five years?" "Tell me your life goals for and how you see this company helping you achieve them."

3) Benefits - Let the candidate hear your vision, your passion, and benefits of joining your team

A. Write out the benefits and the drawbacks of the job opportunities that you have available. It's very important that you highlight all of the positive aspects of your job opportunities and that you deal with all of the potential reasons someone would not want to come work with you during this first interview. If you're too young to look credible in the interviewee's eyes, bring it up and deal with this potential objection. If your business is in a niche that potential candidates find to be less than exciting, bring it up and deal with this potential objection. If your website looks super crappy, or if you have a massive stain on your shirt, bring it up and deal with this potential objection during this interview. You goal is to convince "A Players" to come and join your team. "A Players" always have many job opportunities to choose from so your pitch must be compelling. You can't just show them your brochure and your opportunity and believe that they will just naturally get as excited about the job as you are. You must craft out a presentation that allows you to share your company's BIG VISION in a compelling way over and over again when speaking with new candidates.

B. Example, "At DJ Connection we are going to open up a wedding mall in every major market in the country over the next ten years. We started in a dorm room, and have averaged a 20% annual growth rate since that point. We have grown because we have a *Big Vision*, uncompromising standards and great team of devoted people who are willing to work hard to turn this *Big Vision* into a *Big Reality* that pays them *Big Pay Checks*."

4) Call to Action - Make sure that every interview ends with an appropriate call to action

  A. Script out the call to action that you will use every time at the end of your interviews.

  B. Example, "Well, Neil Diamond, do you have any additional questions for me? Well here is our next step. We are going to need for you to shadow one of our top employees at work for one day so that we can see if you will be a good fit for our team. We have super-high standards, and we want to make sure that you are the kind of guy that would wow our customers. Do you want to shadow on Friday or Saturday?

To make it in business, you are going to have to be able to attract customers and people to work with you. The people in this world that organize large amounts of labor for the achievement of a common objective will make uncommon and *Huge Sums* of money. The people in this world that don't like people and who cannot organize large amounts of labor for the achievement of a common objective are destined to work for those who can. Decide right now that you will be person who likes people and who is up to the challenge of hiring, inspiring and managing large numbers of humans! You can do it!

  "The ability to deal with people is as purchasable a commodity as sugar or coffee and I will pay more for that ability than for any other under the sun." John D. Rockefeller (the founder of Standard Oil and once the world's wealthiest man)

**Hiring people that have great attitudes and great expectations for their lives is absolutely critical to your success, however it is very hard to find these people if you don't know how to systematically do this. If you need help writing effective "help wanted" advertisements, Facebook posts, and other effective recruitment tools, do not hesitate to call us today. Unfortunately en route to winning the U.S. Small Business Administrative "Entrepreneur of the Year Award" and countless other honors, we discovered nearly every ineffective employee recruiting strategy out there. Save yourself the time and frustration and call us today. We will help you design an effective recruitment strategy that change the face of your business quickly. Be a pirate not a pioneer. If you need help, call us today at (918) 851-6920 or contact us via our website at www.MakeYourLifeEpic.com.

Bonus Profound Truth: Leadership

People will only follow someone who is more self-disciplined than themselves.

"As I grow older, I pay less attention to what men say. I just watch what they do." - Andrew Carnegie (Steel Mogul and one of the World's Wealthiest Men of All Time)

When you are at the top you are held to a higher standard than others. I love the tattoo worn by countless athletes that reads, "Only God can judge me." And yes that is true from an eternal perspective. But on the planet Earth, people will judge you regardless of what your tattoo says. People will judge you based on what you do, not based on what you intend on doing. This is harsh. But this is the truth. I have included this Andrew Carnegie quote in my book a few times, not by mistake but to emphasize a point. If you are going to be a leader, you are going to need followers. If you are going to attract followers, people must judge you as "being worth following". If people think you don't have your finances, your emotions, your actions and your life together, they are not going to want to follow you. If you are going to be successful as a leader you must begin following these five leadership rules immediately.

Leadership Rule #1 - Model the behavior you want to see out of others. If you want people to be on time, be on time. If you want others to work without complaining, then work without complaining. Hold yourself to a higher standard than your people and the people around you will begin to improve their behavior as well.

Leadership Rule #2 - Remember we are managing humans here, not robots. The late great success author Dale Carnegie once wrote, "When dealing with people, remember you are not dealing with creatures of logic, but with creatures of emotion, creatures bristling with prejudice, and motivated by pride and vanity." You must take the time to get to know your people and what motivates them if you are ever going to motivate them.

Leadership Rule #3 - Only speak positively when awake. When you are in front of others you must always speak positively. If someone has wronged you or I, we must not speak of it out loud. This rule is tough for me to live by. However, the more business deals you get involved in, the more you will get wronged. Thus, this law will continue to grow in importance over time. If you are a business owner, you are a leader and your words will often carry more weight than you think they do. Trust me, I know what it feels like to be wronged by an employee or to have items stolen by a member of your team. Whether this is fair or not, our words are heavier than others. If a new employee says, "That jerk in accounting is out of their mind!" That is not good. If the leadership of a company says, "Those guys in accounting are out of their minds!" This is awful. As leaders, our words can convey a deep meaning to our people. If a leader talks poorly about an employee, next thing you know the entire team is speaking negatively about all the employees. Carry a mirror and watch your mouth.

Leadership Rule #4 - You must always be improving upon yourself. The people who work for you or with you do so because they see something in you that they admire. If they don't see something that they admire, and if you fail to inspire, they will soon lose their desire to be a part of your empire. Get it? Improve yourself constantly and your team will stay loyal. Devote so much time to self-improvement that you couldn't possibly find the time needed to criticize others.

Leadership Rule #5 - "Where there is no vision, the people perish." - Proverbs 29:18. If you don't believe in the Bible, here is the secular translation. If your company is not growing your top people will be going. If your people don't see the dream, then they are quitting your team. If your staff doesn't see the goal they are going to lose their soul (that one might have been a little dramatic). My friend, people are not going to stick around and work for a company that is not going anywhere. Most people won't even wait in a drive-thru line for more than five minutes and in today's microwave society. People are not going to stick around a stagnant company for very long.

*****

Bonus Profound Truth: Enthusiasm

You must be able to create your own momentum.

"I would rather hire a man with enthusiasm, than a man who knows everything." - John D. Rockefeller (Oil Tycoon, the world's best manager and richest man during his time)

The word enthusiasm comes from the Greek word, *Theos*. Now, I am not a Greek scholar, however I did find it interesting when I discovered that the Greek word *Theos* means "God within." Basically, enthusiasm means to talk with so much energy and passion that it appears God is within you. Although that might be a little hard to do (and you probably don't have a long enough beard to pass as a deity), we can all certainly bring enthusiasm to everything we do. Enthusiasm is the magic spark that starts a fire within an organization. We have all heard a basketball or sports announcer say, "He's on fire!" when referring to an athlete who is "in the zone" and simply cannot be stopped at that given time. I believe bringing enthusiasm to the workplace, puts you "in the zone" at the workplace. Personally I have no place for managers in my business who cannot motivate themselves and others with enthusiasm. Fair or not, the American consumer also has no room in their budget to buy products and services from passionless companies.

Today it might be hard to see, but Wal-Mart started out as one man's dream to lower the cost of goods and the overall cost of living for every American. When Sam Walton had those thoughts, he did not wish they would come into fruition. He spoke to his mountains with conviction and enthusiasm. He made them move. Sam started his first retail store and then promptly lost it all because his landlord would not renew his lease. One poorly written agreement later, he was out of business after having invested all of his money and time. But

Sam did not quit. He enthusiastically got back up and fought for what he wanted.

When P. Diddy / Puff Daddy / Sean Combs (that guy) started out interning for a record label while attending Howard University, he did not just show up. The man became legendary for the enthusiasm he brought the table everyday as an intern and promoter. P. Diddy breathed life and spoke confidence into the lives of Mary J. Blige, Christopher Wallace (Notorious B.I.G.), Mase, Carl Thomas, 112, Jodeci, and the countless acts he developed. If Mr. Combs worked without a passion and without the "eye of the tiger" he would not be the huge success he is today.

When Howard Schultz got the crazy idea to open up a Starbucks on nearly every major street corner it did not all come easy for him. He brought passion and energy to work every day for years to convince us all that we wanted a coffee experience and not just a Styrofoam cup filled with a marginal cup of coffee. He spoke with enthusiasm as though he had the conviction of God within him. Howard didn't listen to doubters who thought $4.00 cups of coffee would never work. He made it work. He won over Americans with his passion. As Winston Churchill once said, "Success in life consists of going from one mistake to the next without losing your enthusiasm."

At the end of the day, people with enthusiasm get things done. People without enthusiasm "try to get things done if they can" and they never do. If you want to be successful you have to bring enthusiasm to work every day. Isn't it wild that Rockefeller, the world's richest man during his time and the world's largest employer of his time commented that he would rather hire a man with enthusiasm than a man who knew everything? Think about that. Would he have wanted to hire you?

*****

Chapter 9:
Raising Capital

There Is Always An Abundance of Capital and A Shortage of
Good Ideas Good Ideas Worth Investing In.

*"There is always plenty of capital for those who can create
practical plans for using it"* - Napoleon Hill

O ver the years, countless established entrepreneurs and
would-be entrepreneurs have come to me in search of
capital. They've asked me for it in a variety of ways ranging
from, "Dude, I really need some money" to "Do you know
people that have money?" to "How does somebody go out
there and get a small business loan?" to "I have a way for you
to make a 30% on your money every month for the rest of your
life if you invest in these bottles of Mona Vi." These are all
valid questions; however I recommend that you would never
utter the phrase, "Dude, I really need some money." Raising
capital has never been a problem for me, and it will never be a
problem for you if follow my proven system. If you don't
follow my seven-part system, I can't help you.

Step 1: Make yourself qualify

In our world of "artificial and politically correct equality," we have a belief everyone has the right to qualify for the loans and capital "they need". If nothing else, the financial ups and downs that our country endured under Bush / Obama should have taught everyone that giving loans to "everyone with a pulse" is probably not a good idea. When people have bad credit, it's usually because they made bad decisions repeatedly until they could no longer service their debt. It doesn't mean they are a bad person, it just means they are bad at managing their money. Would you want a super mean human teaching kindergarten classes? "Oh Clay, but that is mean!" Really? Is that mean, or that real? Andrew Carnegie once famously wrote, "As I grow older, I pay less attention to what men say. I just watch what they do." His statement ultimately validates my "Making Yourself Qualify" formula. Here it is, "Your Reputation + Practical Education = Level of Compensation (Investment Dollars)." Let's take a brief second to break that down like a car with an exploding driver-side wheel.

Your reputation:

This is a statement of where you are right now financially and personally. If you are financially destitute and you are spiritually and emotionally bankrupt no one will be willing to invest in you. If you are financially destitute, but you are an outstanding person and you have a reputation for showing up early, leaving late, being a person of detail, thrift, uncompromising integrity, energy, enthusiasm, resourcefulness, and zeal, you might get the money. If you are a person who has been financially successful with the limited resources you have had, and you have a reputation for showing up early, leaving late, being a person of detail, thrift, uncompromising integrity, energy, enthusiasm, resourcefulness, and zeal, you will get the money capital you need. If you want to raise capital, get to work on yourself right now, because you might not qualify right now on a human or financial level.

Step 2: Your business plan must be explainable to your significant other, to laymen, to investors and to anyone with a functional brain with thirty seconds. From a general and broad vision casting perspective, you must be able to quickly intrigue and peak the interest of a room full of people, with the problem your product / service solves you must be able to quickly explain how you will charge for it, who your potential customers are and how you can prove that there is truly a demand for the product / services you are describing. If you cannot do this, you will not raise capital. You simply cannot have an idea that takes people one hour to grasp if you are going to convince them to invest in your business. You must be able to *Wow* your audience from a topical perspective if you are going to have any chance of winning them over.

George Lucas, the creator of *Star Wars,* made detailed models of the ships and vehicles in the movie and he even went as far as hiring an artist to paint a huge background for one of the scenes to convince Hollywood investors that his ideas were truly more than just an artistic whim. He had to convince the Hollywood studios that his plan had been thought out to the point where capital was the final detail he needed. He knew and you need to know that investors don't want to have to help you with your business. Investors want their money to work for them. Most investors only want money to work as an accelerator for an existing and proven business model that works. They just want to provide you with the capital you need so they can make the return on their money they need.

My friend, invest the time in putting together a dynamic presentation that is visually stimulating. Tell a story and wow your audience. If you don't like public speaking and giving presentations then you won't like raising capital. If you get nervous, join the club. You are not alone. If you have a functional brain you probably should be a little nervous when you are involved in a conversation that has the potential to change the direction of your life forever. Unless they don't have a soul, most men should be a little nervous when the propose to the woman of their dreams. However, pretty safe to say that no one is going to wake up with an all-consuming passion and desire to give you the money you need and want to grow or start your business. You must passionately convince people that your business plan is worth investing in. I personally think it is super fun and exhilarating. If you are not a creative person, find someone who is to help you. However, once again, keep this in mind: If your ideas do not *Wow* them within the first thirty seconds your presentation is over, regardless of when you finish talking. Trust me on this. I was shot down time and time again during my early career. And it was nearly always because I failed to plan out a "wow moment" during the first thirty seconds of my presentation.

Step 3: You must be able to prove all of the assumptions you made with facts. You have probably been on the planet long enough to hear the phrase, "Don't say anything you can't prove." This is what I am about here. It is absolutely critical that every claim you make can be supported by a fact that clearly proves the truth and merits of what you are saying. If you are saying something that is not provable, you will not get the investment dollars. You will be laughed at, or you will be called a liar. Bottom line, there is no room for puffery in a business presentation or in life. Be real with yourself and the people you are trying to wow.

Remember most people who "earned" their wealth achieved success through the careful implementation of a strategy and a plan that they had to be smart enough to create. These people are resourceful, smart, and sharp as a tack. They are not going to just believe every statement you make. In fact, the holes they easily shoot in your presentation will ultimately help you secure the most. These people have been around the block and they know where the holes are in your thinking. They know where your biggest bottlenecks will be and are currently. You want them to tell you why it won't work. Their ideas are worth millions, which is why they have millions to invest. If they poke a hole in your plan, ask them for the best way to fix your "business boat" so that it doesn't sink. Don't get bitter. Get better. You have to promise yourself that when this moment arrives you will ask these investors, "what could I do better?"

Step 4: You must have a detailed pro forma / costing sheet to present to them that clearly explains to them in a detailed, specific, itemized, and analytical way where every dollar that will come into your business will go. These sheets normally take me and our team thirty hours to make. They are awful and they seriously make me want to sucker punch a cute baby Koala while simultaneously stapling my forehead. The process of making these is mind numbing and you really need to hire a "numbers guy" to help make this document. You literally must account for every dollar that will come into your business. You must show how every dime will be used. Your investor wants to know that you have accurately accounted for taxes, insurance, random-acts of badness, realistic sales numbers, bad economies, debt-service, credit card payments, labor costs, payroll tax costs, office lease expenses, furniture, infrastructure, moving costs, janitorial expenses, marketing materials, etc...*Everything* must be on these sheets!

**If you need help with making a document like this, contact us today. Through the process of creating of these documents we have actually saved entrepreneurs thousands of dollars per month. It's seems crazy, but as your company grows you will break the bank $5 at a time. You'll overspend here. You'll create a staffing redundancy there. And at the end of the month, you won't come out ahead. In fact, the more focused on growth your small business is, the more you will tend to neglect accounting.

Step 5: You must possess the "unyielding faith" that John D. Rockefeller always spoke so much about during his time. Rockefeller believed that a person must possess perseverance, unyielding faith, and enthusiasm in order to succeed. I agree. However, if I didn't agree I would still listen to him over me anyway because was the world's richest man. You must go into presentations looking sharp, acting sharp and believing that you will achieve success. You must fake it before you make it. You must have the "fire in your eyes." Investors must be able to see the determination, the drive and the fight boiling up inside you when they look into your eyes. Investors must feel the integrity flowing through you when they shake your hand. Business moguls and successful entrepreneurs must be inspired by your confidence. You must inspire confidence. If your demeanor and your overall look inspires doubt, you need to work on steps one through four again. The more details you know, the more confident you will be. You must know your business plan and your business industry better than anyone else. You must feel comfortable with sharing your vision and you must be able to support what you are saying with provable facts.

Step 6: Make sure that investing in your business is a "no-brainer" for any potential investor. Make the returns on invested capital so good and so strong and so fair that it really wouldn't make sense for them not to invest. Private investors are going to want to make at least a 10% return on their money or they are not going to want to invest in you. If they just put their money in the bank they will at least make a 2% or 3% return on their money. If they invest with you, they do not have the guarantee that their funds will be there (like they think they do at the bank).

When they invest in you, you will introduce considerably more risk into the picture. For this added risk, they will expect a considerably higher return on their money. Remember these *Investors Are Not Excited To Lend You Money And They Are Not Passionate About Your Ideas, They Are Passionate About Making A Return On Their Hard-Earned Money.* Make sure that you present your ideas in a way that truly create a WIN for them and a WIN for you. Point out these Wins, time and time again. Don't fool yourself. These people are not excited about your ideas. They are excited about making lots of money in a passive way by funding your ideas.

Step 7: Stay out of the banks if possible as a start-up. As an entrepreneur you must be able to get things done quickly. Banks specialize in taking a long amount of time to do anything to make sure that every decision is wise decision. Banks want you to share your ideas with the Vice President, the President, and with the Board. Banks want you to present, present, and present some more. Banks want you to give them a 20% deposit. Banks want you to update them with financials once a month after you get the loan. Banks want you to spend six months going through the loan approval process. Procrastination always leads to diminishing motivation and the acceptance of your situation. Furthermore, banks are becoming more and more bureaucratic because of the increasingly intense government regulations surrounding the lending industry. You will start out being excited and after spending seven months with some of these banking yahoos (some people in the banking industry are not yahoos) who have never run a business before you will be so filled with doubt and negativity that you might begin to have doubts about what gender you are, and what your religious faith is. My friend, nearly all start-ups have been funded by capital raised from family, friends, associates, personal savings, credit cards, home equity lines etc.... Just stay out of the bank when trying to startup a business. Nearly all banks are not entrepreneurial. To build your faith on the concept of raising capital from family and friends, just read the examples below:

- David Green, the founder of billion dollar Hobby Lobby craft store chain started his company with an initial investment of $600.
- Warren Buffet began aggressively growing his investment fund (at the age of 30) by asking one of his partners, a doctor, to find ten doctors who were willing to invest $10,000 each in his partnership. Eventually eleven agreed, and Buffet pooled their money with a mere $100 original investment of his own.
- Sarah Blakely, the founder of the billion dollar SPANX company funded her startup with $5,000 she had in savings.
- Sam Walton, the founder of Walmart started one of the world's largest companies with the help of a $20,000 loan from his father-in-law, plus $5,000 he had saved from his time in the Army.
- Conrad Hilton was saved from bankruptcy and losing his entire hotel chain by a $25,000 investment from his mother Mary.

- Mark Zuckerburg started Facebook with the help of an initial investment of several thousand dollars from his fellow Harvard classmate Eduardo Saverin.
- Steve Jobs and Steve Wozniak started Apple out of Steve's parent's garage. Steve was 16 and Wozniak was 21 when they first met.
- Larry Page and Sergey Brin started Google while working on a research project at Stanford University. They started the business using every spare dollar they had on hand, until they were finally able to secure a $100,000 investment from Andy Bechtolsheim, co-founder of Sun Microsystems. Bechtolsheim invested the money into their company before they were even "officially" incorporated.

Once your business has been established and is booming, every bank in town will reach out to you to "Come and join them at the local bank, where they treat every customer like family," etc....Banks want collateral. Banks want to be able guarantee that you will pay them back and 95% of the entrepreneurs I talk with don't have a way to guarantee this. Most entrepreneurs I know have $10,000 or less and a bunch of drive. They have good credit scores and they come from a modest background and they have been diligent with what they have. They have managed their money well, and they have begun to generate resentment with contentment. They have a skill and they are confident in their abilities to support themselves using their skills. However, they don't have the collateral in place to secure a loan. My friend, you are not alone, but most banks will make you feel like you are. For the most part, entrepreneurs don't work at banks. They start banks, but they do not work at banks. Banks employ people that are can be counted on to follow the rules and systems. Banks employ people that are paid to think "inside the box." As an entrepreneur your whole existence revolves around thinking "outside of the box."

John D. Rockefeller went around town trying to secure capital from everyone in Cleveland with a pulse to turn his big ideas into a big business. Sam Walton borrowed money from Helen's (his wife) family to get Wal-Mart growing. Sam borrowed money from his brother. Sam borrowed money from every human he met with a pulse. This is how a *Big Business* starts. Google was started by Larry and Sergey working out of their dorms at Stanford. They used spare computer parts, all-night hours spent working diligently and eventually capital from an angel investor to get started. I almost do not know of any stories that involve a start-up first going to the bank to secure funding. Most banks only want to lend to proven ideas to help them grow faster. They want to bet on a proven winner. Get scrappy. Get your presentation refined. Get your facts in order. Build your case. Build your pro forma and costing sheets. Get your visual aids built. Then get your capital and getting moving.

If this process seems over-whelming to you, we can help you, however as you can imagine we are always overrun with requests for this type of business consulting. Everyone needs capital right? If you would like to schedule a time for our team to sit down with you to help you build your case and your fund-raising presentation visit: **www.MakeYourLifeEpic.com and then contact us from the site. For more information about great ways to raise venture capital read the autobiography of Sam Walton, *Made in America.*

*****

Three Books

The Three Books Every Entrepreneur Must Read

No matter where in the country I may be speaking or consulting at any even time, I am always asked, "What are the books that every successful entrepreneur has to read?" Candidly, to be successful you must never stop learning, however you must start somewhere and you must have the basic foundation in place if you are ever succeed. You must study successful people and businesses if you are going to be successful. In the world entrepreneurship it's better to be a pirate than a pioneer. In order to see life from the correct perspective, you are going to need to improve your vision. These books will help you improve your vision. It's sad when people aren't blind, but yet they lack vision.

Think and Grow Rich written by Napoleon Hill - This book is the number one self-help book of all time. If you read it and implement the action steps in it you will become rich.

How To Win Friends and Influence People written by Dale Carnegie - If you can't win friends and influence people, you are going to spend your life living in your Mom's basement playing video games with a bunch of unemployed bloggers. Read this book, implement the principles found in the book, and watch your life improve.

The E-Myth by Michael Gerber - Every entrepreneur must have two skills, the skill of solving problems by creating products and services that people are willing to pay for and the skill of building duplicatable and scalable business systems. Read this book. Apply its principles and watch the magic happen.

But, what if you don't like studying successful people?

You will be poor.

The time will never be just right, you must act now.

Your seeds of success won't grow unless you plant them. Intentions won't produce the results you want.

CPSIA information can be obtained at www.ICGtesting.com
Printed in the USA
LVOW052108070612

285040LV00002B/3/P

9 781937 829377